New Orleans

NEW ORLEANS: AS THE WORLD'S GREATEST PORT

BY JOHN H. BERNHARD, C. E.

Transportation Engineer

PUBLISHED BY THE

NEW ORLEANS ASSOCIATION OF COMMERCE

JUNE, 1921

NOTES AND CORRECTIONS

Sources. Since in using facts an author becomes equally responsible for them as he is for his deductions, I feel no need in listing, at the risk of overlooking some, the sources of the facts used.

Thanks are due to a number of public spirited citizens who helped me in my work, the Association of Commerce, Goverment officials and not least, the disabled soldiers and pupils with their leaders of the Delgado Trades School of New Orleans who printed this work.

Dock Board. The first four chapters were published in New Orleans newspapers during the months of June, July and August. By the end of September a new Dock Board was appointed, which new Dock Board named a general manager. Therefore and because the personnel of this new Board and its general manager give abundance of reasons to anticipate the cleanest and most efficient and business-like port administration and management, most of the remarks about the New Orleans Dock Board have only a historic value.

Corrections

Page 11, eight lines from the bottom, figure "270," should read "290."

Page 27, fifteen lines from the bottom, "corrected" should read "correct."

Page 33, eighteenth line from the top, "commercial" should read "economical."

Page 35, ninth line from the top, "nine" should read "ten."

Page 36, seventeenth line from the top, "billion" should read "million." Twenty-fourth line from the top, "nine" should read "ten."

Page 41. In appointing our present Dock Board relieved from his promise to re-appoint the old Dock Board, the Governor did prove that he fully appreciated the magnitude of his decision.

Page 54, insert between the thirteenth and the fourteenth line from the bottom: "7 million square feet, and when our harbor is fully developed".

Page 76, seventh line from top, "Grand Coupuore" should read, "Grand Coupure."

Page 80. The Yumiden lock in Holland has doubled gates.

Page 81, third line from top, "nine" should read "eight".

FOREWORD

Many pre-war trade routes and methods are abandoned.

The World War closed an old, and opened a new era of world's commerce: before, Europe was the Capitalist, the United States and Russia its Farm, the Southern Hemisphere and the Far East its Planter.

Conditions have changed between Europe and the United States, and Europe now finds that, after a destruction to the amount of 300 billion dollars, a sum in excess of the total value of the entire United States, it must, without money, laboring under heavy tolls to the United States, compete with the United States for the business of the balance of the world.

The effects of these changed conditions upon New Orleans are traced in the following report.

OUR FOREIGN MARKETS

Up to the end of the fiscal year 1914, 66% of our exports were agricultural, mineral and forest products. We sold our cotton, fuel, corn, ores and lumber principally to Europe, being paid in finished products, refined articles of consumption, and the use of capital;—as Europe paid the Southern Hemisphere and the Far East, where she received in return plantation products, part of which Europe delivered to us at our shore (to be carried into our interior over railroads largely owned in Europe). Our direct trade with the world other than Europe was small and easily served by the few foreign Steamship lines placed partly at our disposal.

Our trade with South America moved chiefly one way along a triangle — our raw materials to Europe; finished, high-priced articles from Europe to South America; and coffee and the like from South America to our shores—supplemented by European-American S. S. lines.

After the first six months of world carnage, it became clear that the above had forever changed. England would relinquish her strangle hold on high sea shipping and lose her stand as the World's banker, while her Colonies would become in fact, if not in name, independent. These predictions are now facts. Only a victorious Germany could have stayed its beneficial effects for us.

As far back as February 1915, I pointed out before the Memphis Cotton Exchange that after the World War, an industrial or commercial war would be fought. Such war is now on and is being fought on foreign soil for foreign markets. Its heavy artillery is economy.

The markets most easy of access to us lie in the Southern Hemisphere, and our rival is battered Europe. Three great handicaps are in our favor — our comparatively small debt, our juxtaposition to these markets, and the interest due us on our foreign loans.

Great Britain's debt is equal to 35% of her national wealth; Germany's debt equal to 87%; France to 45%; United States to 8%;— in which figures Germany's promise to pay has been discounted. In addition to 4 billion dollars of frozen credits, Europe owes us 12 billion dollars, on which a combined interest of 800 million dollars falls annually due.

The European nations can only repay this from a favorable trade balance. They are now making every possible effort, by intensified, economic cartels, syndicates and otherwise, to regain and hold their prewar place in the World's trade.

During the World War, perhaps 75% of the world's hitherto well anchored foreign trade has been cast loose from its moorings —the commercial structure of years, our bondage and shackles. It has been set adrift and is moving slowly towards its new center and goal — NEW ORLEANS.

While we occupy an advantageous position with relation to the acquisition and retention of foreign trade, it is baneful to our present insistent opportunities, that the manufacturers, bankers and merchants have not marshalled all our energies and wealth to secure and retain that position in foreign trade we are entitled to,—over 16 billion dollars of which is our rightful share, more than half of which should move via New Orleans. This will result in our continued, well balanced prosperity.

That the United States has been able to pile up a trade balance in 1919 and 1920 is not due to our foresight or business sagacity, but to the imperative needs of the exhausted, starved nations. Now with over 4 billion dollars of frozen credits, the end of this "false dawn" is clear. We cannot go on selling where only "paper" is returned. Payment in gold to us by Europe is impractical. As it is, we with 1-16 of the world's area and population have already 52% of the world's gold supply, or about 4½ billion dollars, and it is being shipped from Europe to us now, in the past three months, on an average of 100 million dollars per month, more than 400 million dollars since January 1st, 1921, or more than 4½% of the world's supply of gold.

We must, therefore, turn to those countries that can repay us with raw materials or products we need. Our chances to find such countries in Europe are few.

AUSTRIA, now only ¾ the area of Louisiana, has given up industrially, and even her street railways, gas and electric works cannot any longer be offered in payment for needed food supplies. They are a liability,—an asset no more. Outside of some magnesite, there is nothing that they can export to us.

BELGIUM, with an area less than ¼ of Louisiana, had in 1920 a deficit in trade balance of 2 billion francs—two-thirds of her total importation. She cannot export any commodity that we need

except rawhides, ivory, chemicals, laces, silk thread, linen and crockery—certainly no items of vast import, and even of these, three must be imported from the Congo State.

FRANCE, in area 1-14 of the United States, is handicapped industrially, through destruction and debts, the maintenance of a large Army and Navy, the loss of interest on her investments in Russia and Turkey to the extent of not less than 500 million dollars annually, our prohibition, and the world's necessity to dispense for awhile with the non-essential lux-articles sold by France.

She had a deficit of 16 billion francs in her trade balance in 1920, repetition of which the Government is trying to avoid through import restrictions. This unfavorable trade balance does not include any interest payment on her Government debt to us. Even should Germany **not** fail to pay all that is demanded from her, and France receive her full 52% allotted to her, and not suffer any loss changing the gold marks into paper francs, or through discounts upon the German bonds,—even so, such payments would in no instance meet the cost of replacing the property actually destroyed during the warfare.

In another way, it may be stated that France's share of the actual German indemnity will not be sufficient to pay ½ of the French war loans.

Again, in another way, it can be stated that even if Germany pays France in full, France would still need 25 billion francs annually to meet her budget requirements caused by the war—not to speak of the tremendous additional burdens under which France in the future will be bent, in maintaining an Army and Navy necessary in her belief to collect the money from Germany. The report of the Finance Committee of the French Senate of May 23, 1921 shows that France must borrow 32 billion francs to cover expenditures of this year.

GERMANY, 1-18 the area of the United States, must export for 42 years an average of 1300 million gold dollars annually, which means that her exports must be that amount in excess of her imports.

Germany is, in addition to all of this, loaded with a debt, which in proportion to her population, would be equal to a Federal debt of the United States of 75 billion dollars.

Last year, Germany exported goods at the rate of 1 billion gold dollars, consisting of cold-tar dyes, potash, furs, glassware,

4

gloves, musical instruments, sugar beet seeds, toys and textiles. This will have to become 6 billion dollars with only 4 billion imports before she can fully meet her obligations contracted for by the acceptance of the last ultimatum of the Allies. Before the War, her trade balance was about 300 million dollars per year in her favor.

She will, of course, do what she can to secure more than her share of the new trade to be•expected with Russia, as she is even today buying hundreds of thousands of bales of cotton to be directly shipped into Russia. She is now exporting to Russia, at the rate of 10 million dollars a month, agricultural implements, medicines, electrical apparatus, books, clothing, etc.

As far as giving Germany credit is concerned, it must be evident that such credits should be deemed a poor risk and will have to run over periods to be measured only by generations. Germany will be a **competitor** and not a **buyer** from us.

GREAT BRITAIN'S credit is strained. What she can export, ships, woolens, textiles, coal, steel, tin plate, hardware, crockery, paper and rolling stock outside of products derived from her Colonies, we do not need or can manufacture ourselves, with the exception of a few articles which barely can counterbalance the value of the goods she must get from us, such as cotton, corn, copper, lumber, canned goods, etc.

ITALY, 1-30 in area of the United States, one of the victorious, nations in the War, will have to pay to her Allies alone, (Britain, France and the United States) not less than 360 million dollars annually substantially $\frac{1}{4}$ of the sum required of Germany.

40% of its total national income is now extracted by the Government in taxes; and Italy lacks all the raw materials which are the basis of prosperity and the mother of the industrial world. Her raw silk, olive oil, cheese, preserves, fruits, coral, marble, art objects, and sulphur must try to balance her importation of all raw materials.

In the pre-war days, Italy had a trade balance against her of a little more than 200 million dollars, but this was overcome by the wealth brought in by returning immigrants and tourists.

POLAND has a 57 billion Polish mark debt, and 7 million Polish mark gold. The raw materials she can export, we export too. She surely cannot be a great customer.

The same is true of Servia, Czecho-Slovakia, Greece, Turkey, Portugal and Roumania, unless we are willing to accept credit

paper in payment for our products. Holland, Denmark, Sweden, Norway, Spain, and Switzerland are the least impaired remnants of our European markets.

Even the much heralded Termeulen plan is a solution based only on further credits with same supporting arguments as favor Bottomry. It may feed starved nations but can not restore Europe's trade balance.

The only possibility of a substantial but temporary increase of trade with Europe would be through the sale of the German war bonds by France, England, Italy and Belgium to the United States, but where we have already a 16 billion dollar claim upon Europe, can we be willing even if it were possible to us—to buy these German war bonds to any appreciable degree, associated as they must be with the idea of forcible collection? To my mind, the answer is a definite no, unless the German bonds be offered to us at such a discount that they can be bought for speculative purposes, and the speculative element certainly cannot absorb a very large portion of the 34 billion dollars German bonds.

In this connection, I quote here the statement of the Pan-German Deutsche Zeitung, of May 11, 1921: "The acceptance of the ultimatum of the Allies was a question of expediency, but the document should be looked upon as but a scrap of -paper." Germany will evade her obligations so far as it is safe to do so, and so long as this feeling is general, there can be no quotation for her reparation bonds.

Again, where first-class Railroad bonds in this, our country, go begging, with an interest yield of 7%, what will we offer for the 5% German bonds?

One should not forget either, the right of the Allies under the Treaty of Versailles, to discriminate against German exports for five years.

In buying further European investments, consideration will be given to such statements as voiced in the House of Deputies of France, on May 21st, 1921, that "France has a right to refuse the London pact (which was accepted by Germany in accepting the Allies' recent ultimatum), just as the United States refused to ratify the Versailles Treaty." This declaration was received with delirious applause and unprecedented enthusiasm by deputies of all parties.

There are eighty out of one hundred chances that France will repudiate the London agreement as soon as it finds that

even with the now promised payments of Germany, it cannot remain solvent. As a result of all this, leading bankers were cautioned in the last week of May by our President, against further European loans.

Of course, there is in Europe a selling market left for us in Russia, but this must be looked upon as a market of the future, and remotely so, considering first, **our** information of the Russian situation, and secondly, the chaos of Russian affairs. We may do some business with Russia, with whom we are at peace, through the aid of Germany, with whom we are still at war, but this shall not be in a great volume.

Yet there is a great deal of foreign trade available for us, but we have to look for it in other parts of the World. The total world's commerce in the fiscal year ending June 30th, 1914, was 47 billion dollars. Austria, France, Germany, Great Britain, Italy and Japan did 40% of the world's trade. In the year ending June 30th, 1920, our imports were to the amount of 5¼ billion dollars, and our exports 8¼ billion dollars.

Our foreign trade for the years 1918–1919–1920 ran as follows:

IMPORTS FROM

	1918	1919	1920
Europe	13.97%	12.04%	23%
North America	31.18%	35.00%	33%
South America	19.26%	18.16%	12.15%
Asia	28.05%	26.04%	22%
Oceania	4.96%	6.14%	7%
Africa	2.58%	2.62%	2.85%
	100.00%	100.00%	100.00%

EXPORTS TO

	1918	1919	1920
Europe	63.04%	64.15%	54%
North America	20.89%	17.88%	13%
South America	5.31%	5.55%	18%
Asia	7.56%	8.36%	8½%
Oceania	2.28%	2.88%	3½%
Africa	.92%	1.18%	3%
	100.00%	100.00%	100.00%

TABLES SHOWING UNITED STATES IMPORT TRADE FROM LATIN AMERICA FOR 1920.

TABLE A.

Divisions	1920
Latin America	$1,766,993,859
Canada	614,333,652
Rest of America	42,967,424
Europe	1,227,842,145
Asia and Oceania	1,476,765,937
Africa	150,285,194
All other territories	210,000
Total	$5,279,398,211

TABLE B.
LATIN AMERICA.

Divisions	1919	1920
South America	$ 686,221,358	$ 755,579,749
West Indies	440,505,712	764,547,538
Mexico	148,926,376	180,191,075
Central America	43,149,859	66,675,497
Total	$1,318,803,305	$1,766,993,859

TABLE C.
SOUTH AMERICA

Countries	1919	1920
Argentina	$199,158,401	$207,776,868
Bolivia	2,434,750	10,495,298
Brazil	233,570,620	227,587,594
Chile	82,442,364	120,515,599
Colombia	42,911,409	53,644,022
Ecuador	8,966,435	14,479,903
Paraguay	1,031,414	1,179,992
Peru	33,111,352	63,730,964
Uruguay	15,483,828	33,780,647
Venezuela	32,110,785	22,388,862
Total	$686,221,358	$755,579,749

TABLE D.
WEST INDIES.

Countries	1919	1920
Cuba	$418,610,263	$721,695,905
Haiti	9,705,147	8,973,534
Dominican Republic	12,190,302	33,878,099
Total	$440,505,712	$764,547,538

TABLE E.
CENTRAL AMERICA.

Countries	1919	1920
Costa Rica	$ 6,581,789	$10,133,282
Guatemala	12,115,065	20,076,519
Honduras	7,415,588	8,306,364
Nicaragua	5,496,275	7,971,426
Panama	7,395,029	8,272,586
Salvador	4,146,113	11,915,320
Total	$43,149,859	$66,675,497

9

TABLES SHOWING UNITED STATES EXPORT TRADE TO LATIN AMERICA FOR 1920

TABLE A.

Divisions	1920
Latin America	$1,489,301,742
Canada	984,577,118
Rest of America	78,925,542
Europe	4,466,655,197
Asia and Oceania	1,043,396,041
Africa	165,661,771
All other territories	242,337
Total	$8,228,759,748

TABLE B.
LATIN AMERICA.

Divisions	1919	1920
South America	$433,820,545	$613,460,082
West Indies	313,459,836	581,511,679
Mexico	131,455,101	207,854,197
Central America	55,652,518	86,475,784
Total	$934,387,990	$1,489,301,742

TABLE C.
SOUTH AMERICA.

Countries	1919	1920
Argentina	$155,899,390	$213,725,984
Bolivia	4,771,177	4,573,381
Brazil	114,696,309	156,740,365
Chile	53,121,087	55,310,465
Colombia	24,143,646	59,142,277
Ecuador	7,500,603	12,244,165
Paraguay	894,271	1,813,798
Peru	26,945,191	47,037,128
Uruguay	31,419,669	33,720,550
Venezuela	14,429,202	29,151,969
Total	$443,820,545	$613,460,082

TABLE D.
WEST INDIES.

Countries	1919	1920
Cuba	$278,391,222	$515,082,549
Haiti	16,327,848	19,900,380
Dominican Republic	18,740,756	45,258,750
Total	$313,459,826	$581,511,679

TABLE E.
CENTRAL AMERICA

Countries	1919	1920
Costa Rica	$ 4,920,724	$ 9,887,108
Guatemala	8,391,535	10,202,620
Honduras	7,691,928	15,361,919
Nicaragua	6,694,597	9,542,964 ·
Panama	22,019,316	33,333,155
Salvador	5,934,418	8,148,018
Total	$55,652,518	$86,475,784

It is of special interest that our imports from all the world, except Europe and North America were nearly balanced by our exports to those countries, 2300 million dollars against 2740 million dollars. (1920).

We exported to Europe in the same year 4466 million dollars and only imported 1228 million dollars.

We imported more than thrice as much from countries other than Europe than we did from Europe, although we exported 700 million dollars more to Europe than we exported to all other countries combined.

While all other countries showed a favorable trade balance of 270 million dollars, Europe showed a deficit of 3240 million dollars in 1920.

It is of equal interest to see that 77% of our imports come from parts of the world other than Europe, while 46% of our exports went to the same world parts, although in actual dollars not greatly varying. Thus, we imported from parts of the world other than Europe in the year 1920, 4052 million dollars and exported against this 3762 million dollars, which gave this trade balance

11

against us of 290 million dollars, nearly all of which came from Latin America, as we imported from Latin America in 1920, 1767 million dollars and only exported 1490 million dollars, a trade balance against us of 277 million dollars.

The recent figures issued by the Department of Commerce for the first ten months of our fiscal year 1921, ending June 30th accentuate the statements made above. These figures are:

Exports to Europe totalled (in April)_____$174,645,581
compared with_____ 364,094,160
in April last year; while exports
aggregated (in April)_____$ 69,136,424
against (in April)_____$111,364,889
For the ten-month period exports amounted to__$3,053,315,328
compared with_____4,184,087,642
a year ago; and imports_____$822,352,715
compared with_____$968,937,520
Exports to South America aggregated_____$20,717,814
in April, against___ _____ 47,026,874
a year ago. Imports were (in April 1921)_____ 30,535,087
against (in April)_____ 76,007,952
For the ten-month period exports were_____$487,919,783
as compared with_____ 386,418,623
For the year's imports were_____$442,346,673
against _____ 716,373,697

This unfavorable trade balance against us is still neutralised by Europe selling to us such Latin American securities as it may still possess.

Clearly, the important foreign markets to the United States are those of Latin America.

Latin America has 88 million inhabitants—five times as much as the population of the United States in 1845. When it was predicted in 1847 by an eminent economist, J. D. P. DeBow, at that time living in New Orleans, that in 1890 the United States might have as much as 72 million inhabitants, he was considered a dreamer.

So, where the United States at present has a population equal to say only 1-16 of the population per square mile of Holland, would it seem impossible to assume that Latin America may grow in the future, as North America has grown in the past, in which case it would have a population, when equal to the present population per square mile of the United States of 315,000,000.

12

Latin America has an area of 9,000,000 square miles—a little less than thrice the size of the United States.

The Latin American republics occupy and own ¾ of the 12,000,000 square miles of area which comprise the republics of the New World and have 4-10 of its population.

The United States is of immense proportions, but that should not prevent us from remembering that our entire country, without Alaska, could be set down in Brazil and still leave room for a second New England, New York, Pennsylvania and Delaware.

Latin America is a market worth working for—it is undeveloped it is true, but so was the United States a few generations ago, and is still today, compared to what Europe is. Latin America is our closest market, by thousands of miles. With our shores closed to foreign immigration, and war-weary Europe seeing unprecedented numbers of its inhabitants leaving its shores, it seems evident that it shall not long be true that Latin America has but a population of ten per square mile.

Latin American resources are greater than Europe's and ours. Their mighty forests of precious woods, their tremendous deposits of minerals, their food-stuffs, all so very unlike and different from ours—all of these countless and many undeveloped sources of wealth offer a solid foundation for an equitable exchange between them and our products—the sound basis for a large foreign trade.

Closer, with more resources and less developed, why one can't fail to see that Latin Amercia is a market to work for, and we should be grateful in having been liberated from our European bondage and given the opportunity of trading on equal footing with our neighbors and fellow citizens of the same Hemisphere.

Only in May 1921, the British Chancellor, Sir Robert Horne, explained the British coal strike by the fundamental fact that the United States exporters were under-selling Cardiff coal exporters in Argentina. The best American coal, F. O. B. Baltimore is quoted at $5.60 a ton, while the wages in Great Britian alone amount to $5.25 at mine head. In 1920, America exported into Argentina 1½ million tons of cocl, where in 1913 she only imported 38,000 tons from the United States; while the British coal exportation dropped to 275,000 tons. Better results can yet be secured the moment we force Europe to pay interest on the debt it owes us and refuse to buy German bonds.

13

There has not been enough immigration to turn the resources of Latin America into productivity, as America absorbed the world's output in this direction, but this has now been changed by recent restrictive laws passed by the United States.

There were no steamship lines until comparatively recent years to carry the emigrants economically to Latin America, though the Spaniards began to colonize Latin America about the same time that the British and French and Dutch began to reclaim our country —the Spaniards, only to bleed the gold and silver veins and not to work the infinitely greater resources of wealth. So, development marked time, and Latin America has hardly been touched.

See how our trade with Latin America has increased within the past twenty-five years. In 1895 our imports were only 200 million dollars from Latin America. In 1914, 470 million dollars; in 1920, 1¾ billion dollars, and yet of our total imports in 1895, 27% came from Latin America—now in 1920, 33%. Great Britain developed her exports to Latin America from 150 million dollars in 1913 to 500 million dollars in 1920.

In 1895, we exported 75 million dollars to Latin America; in 1914, 282 million dollars; and in 1920, 1⅓ billion dollars.

Of our total exports, only 9.2% went to Latin America in 1895, and 18% in 1920. Thus, this most undeveloped and least populated section, Latin America, is supplying 33% of our needs and taking only 18% of our production. Only 150 million dollars of these products were shipped to Latin America via New Orleans, that is only 10% of the total exports.

16% of the imports of Latin America came through New Orleans.

In what way the Eastern States of the United States have succeeded in creating this uneconomical and irrational movement is explained in a following chapter. Also, why this is changing now.

It has recently been pointed out that losses from foreign credits in South America are not as great as losses from domestic credits. This simple fact is easily explained in the knowledge that Latin America has products with which it can trade with us (which Europe has not). Whatever may be the future of New Orleans trade with Europe, all the signs show that Latin America is our most promising market, the closest, the most productive, the neediest and the safest.

We can, and have to, get along without Europe; we cannot, and have not to get along without Latin America. The total

domestic trade of the United States last year was 93 billion dollars. Our total foreign trade was 13½ billion dollars, or about 14% of our domestic trade. We cannot get along without foreign trade. All of the elements required to control and expand our commerce are at our command.

Is it unreasonable on our part to assume that the American business man is capable of taking, and is going to take, advantage of this unprecedented opportunity? Am I too optimistic in assuming that the opportunity being given, the necessity being there, that our trade with Latin America will develope rapidly, at least as much in the future as our trade has developed in the past?

Is it a sufficient tribute to American pride to let Latin America drag eighty years behind the United States in their estimation? Should I make this period larger, or are we justified in assuming that our Southern neighbors can, under more modern developments and with more economical agents of transportation duplicate our past developments, where they have a territory, thrice as large as our own, and certainly not poorer in raw materials and mineral products?

· The combined twenty-one Latin American Republics export products greatly different from European and our products. The most important are:

Animal Products: hides, furs, skins, feathers, hair (horse), wool, horns, frozen meats, lard, butter and tallow. Fruits: Alligator pears, bananas, limes, olives, oranges, pineapples and many others. Coffee; cocoa; yerba (Mate); sugar; tobacco; mandioca and beans (Tonka); Nuts: cocoanuts, ivory, cohune and copra; oils: copaiba, castor and palm. Lumber: cedar, greenheart, ironwood, lignum-vitae, mahogany. Rubber: gum and balata. Chemicals: Annato, Balsam of Peru and Salvador, castor seed meal, chicle, cocoa, cinomic acid, chincona, copaiba balsam, dividivi, fustic, guano, glycerin, indigo, ipecac, logwood dyes, mangrove bark, medical plants, nitrate, petigrain, quinine, sarsaparilla, tannin, and vanilla. Minerals: aluminum, antimony, asbestos, bismuth, borates, chrone, cobalt, copper, lead, manganese, mercury, nickel, nitrates, phosphates, salt, sulphur, tin, tungsten and zinc. Precious stones, minerals and the like: amber, coral, diamonds, emeralds, gold, mother of pearl, opals, platimum, silver and tortoise shell. Petroleum, asphalt, sponges, fish, hemp, sisal, cocoanut fibre, kapok, mahayo, sandals, straw hats, cement, lime, chalks, marble and clay, gypsum, porfyry.

15

Our total imports of these products is less than the total of imports of the Netherlands in 1913.

Our total exports to these countries is less than ½ of the total exports of the Netherlands in 1913. Yet these Latin American Countries can and do import from us the following:

Arms and ammunition; automobiles and accessories; rubber tires, books, beverages, soft drinks, flour, chemicals, capsules, caustic potash, caustic soda, chemical fertilizers, medicines, clocks, watches, coal, coke, gasoline, kerosine, and all other fuels; cotton piece goods and other dry goods; drugs and patent medicines; surgical cotton gauze and instruments; threads, yarn, cotton, manufactured cotton; electrical machinery; insulators; lamps; wire, etc., explosives; fish; fruits canned goods; grapes; olives; window glass; glass and glassware; iron and steel manufactures like: axles, wheels, cutlery; iron and steel; furniture; enamelware and kitchen utensils; structural steel; locks; nails; bolts; screws; rivets and other staples; stoves; fence materials; tools; typewriters; barbed wire; rubber manufactures; belting, boots, skins; sole leather; agricultural implements and machinery; industrial meters; motors; presses; pumps; textile machinery; bacon; butter; hams; lard; tallow; grease; copper castings; copper plates; ingots; bars; jewelry; galvanized corrugated sheets; lead pipe; lead ingots and sheets; lumber; oak; spruce, pine; tin and tin plates; zinc and plates; bars and sheets; matches; musical instruments; naval stores; oils. Paper and its products; railway material; rice; rubber and its products; scientific instruments; silks; wearing apparel; dried vegetables; hosiery; linen; silk, wool and cotton wearing apparel; hats and caps; furniture; staves; wood of all kinds—soft, plain and veneered; asphalt, garages; celluloid manufactures; cement; chocolate; cordage; jute; hemp; dyes; emery stone and glass powder; ink; bronze; marble; alabaster; meat; paraffin; perfumery; porcelain and other earthenware; sewing machines; soap; starch; tiles; tools and utensils of all kinds; paints; varnishes; wax candles; wind mills; white lead; zinc oxide.

Between these Southern nations, we shall play England's former role. The Argentine Republic for instance is the bread basket of South America. She is not a nation of intense factory output and offers us a splendid market paying us in exchanges and drafts on her neighbors—proceeds of sales of her cereals

and farm products: food supplies to these other South American Republics. We are paying with these drafts our due bills for tropical products.

Not only will New Orleans benefit through the new development of our Latin American trade, but it will also through our trade development with South Africa, Oceania, and the far East, with their spices, tea, lumber (ebony and teakwood) their minerals, chemicals, jute and cordage and matting, seeds and oil, paper and its products; pearls and diamonds, feathers, fans, silk and wool, nuts and fruits.

We must develop these markets one and all; we are going to do so faster than we now can dream, and New Orleans, prepared through its Industrial Canal and Inner Harbor, is going to be an important factor in this speedy developing trade.

EAST AND WEST VERSUS NORTH AND SOUTH MOVEMENT

The first chapter gave proof that our lost trade will not only be replaced by our Latin American trade alone, but stronger, that this Latin American trade, in the very near future, shall surpass our former European trade. This will come to pass in less time than would now be expedient to predict.

The question arises, however, whether it would be safe to believe that such trade will move through Southern Ports in preference to Eastern. Judging by the past, one would reach different conclusions. Think for instance, of the fact, that the Republic of Colombia, far nearer to New Orleans than it is to New York transported last year all its hides through New York, and none whatever through New Orleans. Or again of the 30,000 tons of coffee Columbia exported into the United States, only 2,000 tons went through New Orleans, and the balance 93%, through Atlantic ports.

Where this is true of one Latin American Republic, it is equally true of all others. As much as 87% of the Latin American trade moved in past years, through the Eastern ports, and 70% of the total through New York alone.

This is chiefly due to the manner of development of the United States; secondly, to the artificial, harmful, evil source rate making system that came into being with the development of the railroads; thirdly, to the ever-difficult changing of existing trade-routes; fourthly, to the advertising campaign skillfully engaged in by New York merchants, importers and exporters, who for years have furnished the Latin American merchants with the latest market reports, prices and other information that would guide and assist these merchants in directing their trade to New York.

I wish I could carry you successfully back to North America of the 18th Century. Please picture in your mind that part which eventually became the original thirteen States, as it was at that time. Just see the dignified and placid Virginia and Maryland planter. Do you think he looked upon, what was west of the Alleghanies, in a way materially different from what we now see in South America? Do you fully realize that he but saw, in what is now known as the Mississippi Valley, a vast wilderness of no

18

great importance, and the way he looked upon its denizens then, must have been very similar to the way in which to-day the majority of us look upon Latin America.

Let any American freely talk to you about our Southern neighbors, and you will carry away the conviction that he considers anyone living south of the Rio Grande—certainly those born there —greatly inferior to ourselves; which thought in itself constitutes our greatest handicap toward developing our trade with Latin America.

The New York lawyer, or the New England merchant, of Revolutionary days, had not any broader conception of the Mississippi Valley of its days and its inhabitants.

This has not so greatly changed. A President of one of the greatest financial institutions of Boston, had as recently as 1912, never been west of Lake Placid, N. Y., and had, indeed, a very feeble idea of our great Mississippi Valley.

Don't you then agree with me that his ancestors, these Virginia planters, or New England merchants, had they by any accident read the prediction that some day the Mississippi Valley might hold a population in excess of sixty million poople, that some day this Mississippi Valley may hold the center of population of the United States, its center of commerce,—they would have considered such statements wildly visionary, the hallucinations of a dangerous dreamer.

It thus came about that the United States developed almost solely in the East, only its overflow reaching the West. The people living in the East invested their capital in enterprises around them, with the results that even today, if one draws a line from Milwaukee over Davenport, St. Louis, Louisville, Wheeling, Harrisburg, Baltimore, one will find that 80% of the industries of the United States are located North and East of this line.

Immigration coming from Europe, settled in the East; capital made in the East remained in the East; and only its surplus again, moved westward, slowly following the overflow of its population.

This Eastern capital, with its established banking institutions, with its established merchant houses, naturally drew from the west its trade, laboriously crossing the Appalachian mountains in wasteful disregard of Nature's aid, the easy waterway to the Gulf of Mexico.

19

When later this western country became more developed, it found new barriers against the use of the Mississippi River and its tributaries, in the fact that the mouth of the Missisiippi River was in foreign lands, controlled by foreign laws, made by kings thousands of miles away.

This handicap was removed in the first years of the 19th Century. It was then that New Orleans saw its greatest development, and in 1845 the Mississippi River and its tributaries carried a trade valued at 262 million dollars, equal to 1-5 of the present total Port movement of New Orleans, and 42 million dollars in excess of the total foreign trade of the United States of that year. At that time, the total population west of the Appalachian Mountains was less than 7, million.

These figures stand out more boldly, when thought is given to the fact that in 1845 our total domestic trade was 1½ billion dollars. (In 1895 our total domestic trade was 9 billion dollars against 93 billion dollars in 1920.)

But, just as New Orleans was developing in a way befitting its location, the railroads came into being, naturally backed by Eastern capital and naturally built from the East. Again Nature's dictums were violated, and trade was artificially forced to move from the Mississippi Valley to the Eastern ports, as the at-that-time modern agent of transportation, the railroads, had an easy victory over its contemporary, unimproved Mississippi River, from which even snags were not removed by the United States Government controlled in the East. In this connection read what Judge Hall said in an address before the Mercantile Association of Cincinnati in 1847:

"The (steamboat) trip from Cincinnati to New Orleans and back is made easily in two weeks.........the history of men does not exhibit a spectacle of such rapid advancement in population, wealth, industry, and refinement, such energy, perseverence and enlightened public spirit on the part of individual, as is exhibited in the progress of the western people, nor of so parsimonious and sluggish a spirit as that evinced toward us by the government. We built and maintain a fleet of 500 steamboats bearing annually a freightage of more than $200,000,000; the government on the other hand spent no money at all for our river improvement, withheld from us with a degree of injustice which has scarcely a parallel in the annals of civilized legislation."

20

The map published by the 29th Congress (1845) shows just two railroads running North and South one that ran between Wilmington N. C. to Portland, Me., the other from Cincinnati to Cleveland. On the other hand, there were seven railroads from the Mississippi Valley running almost due east, to Savannah, Charleston, Baltimore, Philadelphia, New York and Boston. The Cincinnati merchant's choice, between shipping his flour by water South, with a 33% chance of having it soiled and spoiled on the unprotected mud banks, called the harbor of New Orleans, subject to a double drayage charge. or, moving it by rail more safely to Eastern ports where his flour had 50¢ per barrel higher value, was an easy one. (Hunt's Magazine, Oct. 1846, Page 355.)

The following quotation is from the "Commercial Review", Vol. 111, Number 1, January 1847.

"But with all her natural advantages, New Orleans has much to do, and which is immediately demanded at her hands. It is not to be questioned by anyone, acquainted with the inland commerce of the great West, that much of this commerce is now already, and a great deal more will be taken from New Orleans to the northern Atlantic seaboard, by way of numerous Canals and Railroads, already in existence, and others that may follow after, and by way of the Lakes."

"Already is there a connection existing between the waters of the Ohio River and the Northern Lakes, connecting with canal, railways, etc. leading to Boston, New York and Philadelphia, and on which produce can be transported to these northern cities as cheap, or cheaper than by way of New Orleans, and without the risk from snags in our rivers. which occasion so heavy insurance, and other objections and injuries to which produce is liable on coming to New Orleans, under the present meagre facilities now offered by the city, for safety, convenience, and saving of expense."

Read the warning of the Chamber of Commerce of New Orleans in 1847, when the Legislature of Virginia passed on the end of February of the same year, an Act to incorporate the Richmond and Ohio Railroads: "When we take into consideration, that all snags, sandbars and other dangers of our Mississippi River navigation are avoided and an insurance of 50¢ a barrel for extra risk for sailing at New Orleans is eliminated, we think we hazard but little in concluding that this route is destined when completed to work a vast change in the movement of our Western produce—

21

add to this the reflection, that this is but **one** of the means resorted
to for the purpose of drawing the commerce of the Western country,
by artificial channels, to the Atlantic border, to say nothing of
the fact that New Orleans, is doing nothing in the way of removing obstacles now in existence, or making any effort to create
for the Western Commerce those cheaper facilities, to insure all or
as much of the produce from the West to seek its market, either
at or through New Orleans. It cannot but be obvious to every
thinking mind, that at least one half of that commerce may be
diverted away from New Orleans to seek a market through other
channels, which otherwise could be rendered tributary in building up her city. Regarding the extent, of the various artificial
means already completed, now in progress, and which are planned,
we find New Orleans has no small opposition to encounter and
overcome, in order to place herself on an equal footing in this
contact for the trade of the Valley of the Mississippi''. It should
be borne in mind, that the people of the Slave States were always
the last, or generally so, in adopting those improvements necessary to facilitate commerce and cheaper transportation from the
point of production to the points of sale or market.

And thus these warnings, to provide New Orleans harbor
with facilities that would ensure safety, economy and dispatch to
commerce in transit, were in vain. But the greatest stress should
be laid upon the fact that we were facing Europe, and New York
vessels had return cargo which the New Orleans vessels lacked.

The exports of 1844 from New Orleans were 54 million
dollars, from the whole country 100 million dollars. The total
imports were 84 million for the country and of which only 5
million dollars entered through New Orleans. Now supposing
that imported goods were as bulky as the raw material sent out
from New Orleans, (which was by no means the case) it appears
that ten vessels out of every eleven that came across the sea,
for the Southern produce, came empty, and therefore this produce had to pay the freight both ways. It is true that some
vessels came with cargoes from New York and Boston, and
brought dry goods, furniture and coffins, but this only shows
that as far as the foreign merchandise was concerned, New York,
Boston with their East and West railroads did the importing.

Then came the Civil War, more disastrous to the South,
with its blockade, Sherman's ''joy ride,'' and destroyed labor

source, than the World War was to Europe; only the World War was fought in Civilization's Parlor, while the Civil War was fought in useful, young, resilient', rich America. A war which was the downfall of Europe would be but a handicap, though a severe one, to this young and vigorous country beaming with energy.

But then after this war, the main part of the Mississippi Valley, financially bankrupt, in economical bondage to the East, could but look on and see the construction of new Eastern and Western railroads, and when finally the North and South lines came into existence, a system of rate making had been adopted that could easily hold down river transportation.

This ever-damned rate making system, connived in by Eastern capitalists and railroad owners whose wants are legalized by the United States Government, shall eventually prove to be America's greatest handicap.

The prime thought of Eastern capital, controlling as it did the capital of the United States, and the sole fiscal agent for Europe, in building the railroads, was development of their private interests, regardless of the interests of the United States.

Thanks to those pork-barrel patriots, we came into the habit of recognizing such basic "principles of rate-making" as "any rate that the traffic can bear," "any rate to beat water competition," "equalizations," "differentials," "classification," "long and short haul:" for strange as it may seem, ridiculous as it may sound, our rail rates are not based upon cost plus profit. Hence as a direct result this ever in volume increasing current of printed "wisdom" issuing forth from this typical American and unique fountain of legal decision, the I. C. C. and with it, in its wake, this endless stream of tariff experts, I. C. C. lawyers.

In a great number of instances, Boston has a lower cost of transportation into Texas than St. Louis; New York a lower one into Louisiana parishes than New Orleans.

The Eastern capitalist not only invested his money in East and West railroads, but new industries were of course located along them.

At that time, too, the Eastern harbors responded splendidly to the shipping needs of that epoch. In contrast with New Orleans, vessels in Boston, New York, Philadelphi and Baltimore, came alongside the wharves on which the warehouses were built— New York had gone to an "enormous" expense in building what

23

was called the "Atlantic Dock", covering a space of forty acres of ground, where vessels could discharge cargo right into the warehouses, and when it was to be reshipped, vessels in like manner came longside and received their cargoes from these warehouses, without subjecting the owner to any charge for drayage or risk of damage from wet.

James Buchanan Eads has just reached manhood, 17 feet at the Pass was New Orleans's threshold. Europe was the forceful world's master.

American shipping had been destroyed and replaced by European lines. Whatever steamship lines we were permitted to use to Latin America, moved from Eastern ports to serve Europe first. The railroads and European steamship lines became greatly dependent upon each other for their East and West freight movement, and nearly all had some working arrangements for freight exchange and co-operation, with unpublished rate rebates, some still in existence, detrimental to the natural development of the Valley.

Here are the factors that have worked against New Orleans, and let us now see what happened to them.

The center of population has moved west of the Appalachians. Capital is becoming stronger daily in Chicago, St. Louis, and New Orleans. Europe is destroyed to the extent of $300,000,-000,000,000, 10% more than the entire value, real and personal, of the United States, The Spaniard of the 18th Century has now made room for a more vigorous race in South America. These new nations are bent upon developing their country, infinitely richer in mineral and agriculture resources than ours, and their future is just as promising as our own was in the early 19th Century.

The Valley and Louisiana are developing, and last but not least, boats have again made their appearance upon the Mississippi River. The railroads are daily giving evidence of change of heart, whether through better understanding or forced through circumstances, and daily our rate structure is undergoing alternation almost invariably improving the situation. The Interstate-Commerce Commission must obey the trend of times, even if walking itself backward, forced onward towards our goal by the surging tide of economic necessities. For instance: An export freight rate parity with New York for the gulf and south Atlantic

ports for freight originating in the region lying north of the Ohio and east of the Mississippi River, has recently been granted. Barges forced this.

The Eastern ports, for the first time in their existence, find themselves on the defense, New York, with her usual foresight, is seeing the writing on the wall. Already in the "Port of New York Annual Report" of this year we can read: "The Port of New York is in danger of losing its vast commerce to other ports". The Eastern ports are attempting now to hold our birthright, not only through great and costly improvements, but also by means of ties, predestined to fail because they are harmful to this nation's economy.

This was the necessity which gave life to the so long requested joint New York–New Jersey State Port Commission. Which gave the strength that started, on the 6th of April of this year, the constuction of the 1600 acre Jamaica Mill Harbor—estimated to cost 125 million dollars, just after the completion of the Erie Canal, at a cost of 155 million dollars.

An old but powerful tie is the 90% ownership or control of New Orleans steamship lines in the East and in Europe, resulting in far more frequent service from New York than from New Orleans to the South. There are 52 S. S. Lines from New York to Latin America, 31 of which are controlled in New York and vicinity, 15 in England and 6 in other foreign countries, while there are 25 S. S. Lines out of New Orleans serving Latin America, 7 of which are controlled in New Orleans; 9 in New York, and 9 in foreign countries.

However, most of these ties are again rates or rate-restriction, such as are maintained through the North Atlantic shipping confereuce, through which the Eastern ports have an opportunity to dictate the Ocean rates on half of the vessels touching New Orleans

This is designed to forestall the possibility that New Orleans should charge rates less than and detrimental to "the Eastern interest". Eastern financial interests, by dominating the shipping conference, have been able to export to Mexican and Central American ports at the same ocean rates as New Orleans. In some cases, the New Orleans rate to Latin America, forced upon us by New York, is higher than from New York, as, for instance, with Cement, which moves for $10.00 a ton from New York to Brazil and Argentine, against a New Orleans rate $14.00 a ton.

These shipping conferences authorized in war times by the Shipping Act, were hoisted upon an unaware South. This Act gives the Shipping Board the right and authority to disapprove, cancel or modify any ocean freight rate agreement. Our sure weapon against this is the tramp steamer, which is now so abundant in the East, but which is a true weather-vane. These tramp steamers will soon flock to our shores.

The unique result of this is shown for instance, in the announcement on May 25, 1921, that, the Mexican Government owned Steamship line, operating to New Orleans, the Compania Naviera Mexicana, preparatory to accepting the proffered New York rate war, would transfer the agency for the Company to the Mexican Consul. Rates from New Orleans to Mexican and Central American ports are the same as from New York on nearly all principal commodities.

Each time Gulf operators have established short route rates, the New York ship operators have met them. New York vessels have even run at a loss, in some cases to maintain their routes and gradually squeeze out the operators from the Gulf ports.

Some day soon, New Orleans may be allowed by the Shipping Board to act independently in fixing rates. At any rate, the Shipping Board's control is irrevocably condemned and will soon expire. This is perhaps the explanation of the fact that a baseball authority was recently appointed its Chairman.

Another established method is by means of "Pittsburgh plus" through which we are denied the advantages of the location of our Southern ore deposits, but must pay a tribute to the East equal to the cost of removing these ore deposits to Pittsburgh. "Pittsburgh plus" is a device of the Steel mills by which all steel sold in the country, wherever manufactured, is priced F. O. B. Pittsburgh. That means, if steel is made at Gary, Chicago, or Birmingham, where they make it cheaper than at Pittsburgh, the purchaser pays the price charged at the mill, plus the freight from Pittsburgh to destination. That is a device by which the Steel mills, controlled in the East, profit to the extent of about 75 million dollars annually for an absolutely fictitious freight charge, and because of it, and to the extent of it, industry in the Valley is hampered.

Still other methods are buried in the Shipping Board, Tariff, Federal Trade Commission, the Interstate Commerce Commission, but all these are merely restraining influence compared to our pre-war shackles. Our greatest liberator from those rates are

barge-lines upon the river, not solely through the actual performance of the barges, but by the effect of their existence upon the rate structure.

The difficult and slow process of changing existing trade routes has been abridged by the War, which upset old routes and now new ones have a better chance. Great stress must be laid upon the fact that with Europe diminished as a market, Latin America looming up, the United States has made "face about" to Latin America and the Southern Hemisphere, and with it the advantages which made New York are now handed over to New Orleans. The west to east movement, long hard to stop, is now a dead momentum, and will swing to North and South.

Economy must aid us in speeding up the movement. Economy in transportation in the true keystone of real economy.

Economy in transportation in the Mississippi Valley points to New Orleans.

Without reason, rhyme or right, by artificial means, New York controlled before 70% of the Nation's trade with Latin America. These artificial barriers now removed, cannot New Orleans hope to duplicate what New York did in the past? If these thoughts are corrected, if my view of New Orleans' future is right, then when the United States sees her Latin American trade grow from three billion dollars to 14 billion in the next twenty years, New Orleans will see her rightful share, or 70% go through her gates: 10 billion dollars of merchandise to Latin America alone instead of one billion to all the World now. Does this sound big? Just think in 1845, the total commerce of New Orleans equalled ¼ of the whole of the commerce of Great Britain. Now Great Britain's foreign commerce in 14 times that of New Orleans.

Stock phrases, such as "New Orleans is the custodian of the Gateway of the Mississippi River and Mississippi Valley" take on new lustre and meaning that now even the "safe" and "practical" business man can understand, and he comes to comprehend, that the Industrial Canal alone can be trusted with the task of economically transmitting this vast new tonnage.

NEW ORLEANS' FUTURE TRADE

The first chapter gave proof of how the current of our foreign trade is changing from an east and westerly direction to a southern and northerly one.

The second chapter. demonstrated that the changing trade stream does not pivot on the Eastern ports, but that the valley shall henceforth be its highway.

Let us now see how much of this trade stream will move through New Orleans.

Like the drainage basin of a river system, a port has as its hinterland a territory for which it acts as drain, as well as means of access.

Such economical drainage basin is chiefly based on rail rates, and with this, on the feeding waterways.

The principal Gulf Ports outside of New Orleans are Pensacola, Mobile, Gulfport, the Sabine District, Galveston, and Houston.

Pensacola is the terminus of the L. & N. R. R. and located on the Escambia River, a short, unimportant river with a channel of less than 6 ft. Outside of the L. & N. there is the never finished Gulf, Florida and Alabama R. R.

The Pensacola territory is largely the eastern part of the one of Mobile and does not in any way tap any field rightly belonging to New Orleans.

The Mobile territory chiefly draws the southeastern boundary of New Orleans' trading basin. It is well served by five railroads, two of which are major systems, the Southern with the M. & O. and the L. & N. In addition to this it has the cheap water routes over the Tombigbee, Warrior and Alabama Rivers. As a result of all this it can compete in rail rates with New Orleans in Memphis, Cairo, Kansas City, St. Louis, Chicago, Louisville and every place east of the Mississippi River. However, thanks to the government barge line, the cities on the Mississippi river and west of it, should always be classified as New Orleans territory.

Gulfport on account of her limited port facilities, open unprotected harbor and the limited railroad connections with the country behind her, can only make a small encroachment on New Orleans' field. Its trade influence should not extend beyond a local field but it did move New Orleans' eastern trade boundary from Biloxi westward to Bay St. Louis.

Gulfport's harbor is almost solely fit and used for lumber export but manages through the total absence of lumber export facilities in New Orleans to substantially cut into New Orleans' share of this business. In the last 10 years, Gulfport exported 3500 million feet'of lumber, reduced last year to 120 million feet. Twenty years ago Gulfport did not count as a harbor and twenty years from now it will not any more. It is even now on a decided decline, but had it not been for lack of import tonnage due to one-man control of its main feeding railroad, it would have been a much more serious competitor. But even today it cuts into distinct local New Orleans territory as for instance Bogalusa and Slidell.

The same story is now about to repeat itself in the Sabine District, Texas. Nine years ago some "visionary dreamer" suggested the making of seaports out of Beaumont and Orange Texas. Today this district including Port Arthur, Beaumont and Orange, exports 65% or about 732,000 tons more oil than New Orleans. But then New Orleans has no oil harbor. The Sabine District is served by the S. P., Santa Fe, K. C. So., and the Gulf Coast Lines and places the western boundary of New Orleans' foreign trade territory over New Iberia, Lafayette, Alexandria and Shreveport.

It is fortunate for New Orleans, unfortunate for the commerce of the United States, that the Sabine River is unimproved and it is equally fortunate for New Orleans commerce that the Sabine River bends to the west., As Gulfport encroaches upon our lumber territory so is the Sabine District eating in New Orleans' oil fields.

Galveston and Houston succeed chiefly through'local Texas railrates in forcing our western boundary line to fight shy of Texas, even denying us the larger share of Oklahoma, yes even Kansas City and St. Louis are cities where Galveston and Houston can meet New Orleans on a parity in railrates. Again due to the fortunate geographical situation of New Orleans and to the **real** use of the Mississippi River, (not its potential. its idle-use) can we claim these cities ours, if we only do not bring the obstructions to economy, called New Orleans "harbor facilities", too much in evidence.

In addition to this we have the fortunate situation for New Orleans that Texas is only **talking** about the **potential** value of water transportation on the Trinity and Brazos River and Inter-

coastal Canal, while the eight railroads serving Galveston and Houston serve mainly the west and northwest. But as it is Galveston makes heavy inroads on our general trade, especiallly our cotton trade, so much so that Galveston's gain in cotton business equals New Orleans' loss.

The northwestern and northeastern b o u n d a r y of New Orleans foreign trade draining basin is dictated by Pacific and Atlantic ports. Taking all this into account, I find that to describe New Orleans hinterland, it can best be divided in three areas. The first: "A", is that part of the valley, the foreign trade of which can hardly be taken away from New Orleans without the consent of its citizens; by merely opposing grossly unfair methods of competition and by seeing to it that the streets do not become entirely impassable, and without similar exhibitions of supine placidness, New Orleans should always be the port for the foreign trade of this territory.

All the points in territory "A" are nearer to New Orleans than any other seaport, except the very northwest corner, which is slightly nearer to Seattle and Portland. This is compensated by the fact that these ports have as barriers the Rocky Mountains. Every place in this territory can be given water transportation to New Orleans or what practically would mean water transportation, that is water and rail.

The foreign trade of the next territory: "B" is also available to New Orleans and will readily yield to any fair courting—and as long as New Orleans remains on equal footing in freight rates and similar factors of transportation, it is almost sure to move the foreign trade of this territory. Barge lines and fair freight rates will make New Orleans master in this field.

There is a third territory: "C" which is highly competitive and its trade can only be had by New Orleans as the fruit of the highest economy and efficiency. That is territory whose natural intent would be to seek other ports than New Orleans, but with true coordination of highly economicallv developed shipping facilities, New Orleans can secure this trade.

Territory "A" is confined by a line commencing just west of Gulfport, Miss., running over Hattiesburg, Meridian, Columbus, to Corinth, Miss., thence over Jackson, Miss., to Fulton, Ky. From there over Paducah, Ky., to Brockport, Ill., Marion, Centralia, Springfield, Galesburg, Rock Island, Ill., following the Mississippi River to Minneapolis, Minn. From Minneapolis it

continues over Elk River, Tergue Falls, Moorehead, Minn., following the state boundary line to the Canadian border, thence the Canadian border to the boundary between Montana and North Dakota, going due south along this boundary line to Colorado. Following the Nebraska-Colorado boundary line to Kansas, from there over Colby, Kan., to Salina, Kan., from where it follows the Arkansas River through Kansas and Oklahoma to the Arkansas boundary thence between Oklahoma and Arkansas to the Red River through this to Alexandria, La., and Lafayette to Houma, La.

This territory has an area of 581,041 square miles, 1-5 of the United States, and a population of 19,355,029 inhabitants, 1-6 of the United States.

Every point in territory "A" has not only New Orleans as its nearest harbor, but every such point can be given the benefit of all or part water transportation to New Orleans. We should carry all its foreign trade, which was in 1919, $22\frac{1}{2}\%$ of the total foreign trade of the United States, or 3 billion dollars, which will become if the reasoning given further is correct, $6\frac{1}{2}$ billion dollars in 15 years from now.

The next territory called "B" is bounded by the same line up to Corinth, Miss., then following the Tennessee River to Florence, Ala., and northward from there just west of the L. & N. Railroad to Clarksville, Tenn. From there over to Hopkinsville, Ky., then north over Columbus, Ind., Indianapolis and Lafayette, Ind., to Chicago, Ill. From Chicago over Madison, Wis., to St. Paul, Minn., to then follow the line "A" to the Canadian boundary; thence following the Canadian boundary to Sweetgrass, Mont., then along the C. P. Railroad to Shelby continuing just west of the Great Northern Railroad via Great Falls to Billings thence to Wyoming border to follow this to the westward around to Encampment, Wyoming after this it goes over Denver, Pueblo, to Trinidad, Colorado, to then follow the Colorado and Oklahoma western and southwestern boundary to Arkansas: through the Red River to Alexandria and from there to New Iberia and Houma, La.

This territory "B" has an area of 991,810 square miles or $\frac{1}{3}$ of the United States and a population of 30 million or 2-7 of the United States.

The foreign trade of this territory is larger than that of territory "A" by 25% of the total of the United States, or in total $47\frac{1}{2}\%$ of trade of the United States, which $47\frac{1}{2}\%$ amounted last year to $6\frac{1}{2}$ billion dollars.

The export and import rates of every point in this territory to New Orleans are in the main, with only few exceptions, equal to such rates to other ports, so that through the effective use of the waterways leading to New Orleans and with economy and dispatch in its harbor, this city can secure a very large proportion if not all of the foreign trade of this territory. In my estimate, I have assumed that New Orleans secures $2/3$ of the foreign trade of this territory (less territory "A") or $2\frac{1}{3}$ billion dollars.

Water transportation is more economical than rail, and the shorter the rail haul and the longer the water haul, over the entire distance from point of origin to point of destination, the greater the economic efficiency. It is the freight rate, not the distance which makes the difference to the shipper.

The boundary line of the third territory "C" commences west of Gulfport, Miss., to Meridian, Miss., York, Ala., to Selma, Anniston, Ala., Atlanta, Ga., Chattanooga, Tenn., following the eastern boundary of Tennessee and Kentucky and West Virginia to Cumberland, Pa. Thence via Pittsburg and Steubenville, Pa., to Columbus, Lima and Toledo, Ohio, to take in all of Michigan, Wisconsin and Minnesota changing line "B" by adding one-half of the state of Idaho the line commencing from Great Falls, Mont., going over Helena and Butte, Mont., to McKay, Idaho: from there to Bailey and Twin Falls, Idaho, to Salt Lake City, Utah: from Salt Lake City to the southeast corner of Utah, going over Green River and Bluff. From there to Santa Fe, New Mexico, Santa Rosa, to Texico, New Mexico, and thence over Plainview, Texas to the Oklahoma border following the Red River; from thence it is the same as line "B".

It has an area of 643,598 square miles in excess of territory "B" or a total of 1,535,408, equal to half of the United States and a total population of 49 million or slightly less than half the population of the United States.

The total foreign trade of territory "C" was last year 63% of the total foreign trade of the United States or $8\frac{1}{2}$ billion dollars, This territory controls the oil and coal production of this country while 70% of the total United States farm products are raised in it. It produces more than half of the nation's cotton, and half of its forest products.

In addition to this, territory "C" produces 4-5 of all the agricultural implements, automobiles and parts, iron and steel, flour and packing house products, 3-5 of all the cement, wagon

32

material and vehicles, dairy products, structural iron, turpentine and rosin, ½ or more of all tiles, coffee roasting, copper-, tin and sheet iron products, machinery and engines, furniture, glassware, lumber, paints and rubber goods.

The total of crops of 1914 in territory "C" was 11 billion dollars, against 16 for the U. S. The total forest products was 2 billion of the four for the U. S. the total mineral products were 3 billion of the five for the whole country, while finally it gave 16 billion of the 25 billion of the U. S. manufactured products. Thus the total of the crops, forest, mineral and manufactured products of this territory "C" was 32 billion dollars of the 50 for the whole U. S for the year ending June 30th, 1914.

Many points in this territory "C" (less territory "B") have ample reasons to ship their foreign trade through ports other than New Orleans and all points have some more or less valuable reason but none need to have with boats upon our rivers and above all with a fully efficient and modern harbor.

I have given New Orleans, when working under such commercial conditions, credit for half the foreign trade of this territory and this half was last year 1 billion dollars.

Let us finally add the possible growth in tonnage, in excess over natural increase, because a larger number of industries shall seek New Orleans, as its greater efficiency and economy as a seaport is proven.

In the past the Eastern ports forced the location of a larger number of industries in territory easily accessible to them, and so should New Orleans in the future succeed in doing. That such increase need not be small can be seen from the fact that even in these depressed times there are being built in the eight most Southern States alone, in monthly average, new factories representing something like six million dollars of investment. This is classified as Territory "E". This does include (a) stopped Eastern development deflected to New Orleans through changed trade routing, (b) natural growth of the Valley, (c) additional growth from elsewhere seeking the new economical Valley location, (d) increased development of the Southern Hemisphere and the far East.

Economic development of the Valley as a unit is a concept appealing and readily grasped. Development of adequate transportation facilities is a need recognised and felt throughout the Valley. Extension of the barge lines and their fullest utilization

means both economical development and transportation economy. Its acceptance, hastened by growth of the "Valley Mind" will insure an additional factor which is going to bring the movement of freight through New Orleans instead of Eastern Ports.

To place American foreign trade on a permanently competitive base with Europe, the process of transportation of raw materials into the finished articles of commerce must be carried on as near as possible to the source of raw material, fuel, and food supply. With an easy route and low cost of transportation, in order to be relieved from congestion and save money, and freedom from embargoes, and through the solution of our transportation problems, railroads and waterways, freight classified under "E" will become heavy because the source of the supply of American raw materials, food, fuel and minerals in this territory called "C".

As a fair example of what special conditions may do in bringing new industries, the cities of Niagara, N. Y. and the country around Keokuk, Iowa, may serve, both forcing the creation of new industries, merely because they deliver cheap power, and thus, when the years of economy have had their effect upon the Valley, this territory "E" will yield an additional 10% even perhaps more of the total foreign trade of this country.

Now adding these figures together, we find that based upon previous arguments, we may expect to see in the future. as soon as we have created true agents of economy around us the following tonnage passing through New Orleans in foreign trade alone, having all the time ignored and left out of consideration any local, coastwise or domestic trade.

All the foreign trade of Territory "A" or 3000 million dollars or 2-3 territory "B" (less territory "A") or 2333 million dollars ½ of territory "C" (less   "   "B") or 1000 million dollars

Total ....6333 million dollars

or 47% of the total foreign trade of the United States based upon last year's statistics. Where New York contrary to true economy, has carried in the past 70% of the foreign commerce of the United States and where now the very causes of this have come to New Orleans, I believe I made a fair estimate in assuming that at the end of 15 years, New Orleans had only done two thirds as well as New York and carried 47% of the foreign trade of the United States.

This would mean that if New Orleans' commerce should amount to 16 billion dollars the foreign trade of the whole United States would have to be about 29½ billion dollars, taking here

34

in consideration the effects of the 10% of territory "E" which by that time will have changed New Orleans' quota to 57% of the foreign trade of the United States.

The total foreign trade of the United States of today is about 13½ billion dollars, 9½ billion pre-war values. Therefore this would be an increase of about 20 billion dollars in 15 years or more than 200% increase in that period.

The domestic trade of the United States increased from 9 billion in 1895 to 93 billion in 1920, in other words multiplied itself nine times in 25 years. The value of manufactured products increased from 24 million dollars in 1914 to 63 billion dollars 1919 or a 160% increase in 5 years.

The total imports of the United States increased in the last five years preceding the war 1 billion 200 million, to 1 billion 800 million, an increase of 50% in five years.

The total exports increased from 1 billion 860 million, to 2 billion 465 million, increase of about 35% in the last five years, preceding the war.

The tonnage that was cleared out of New Orleans increased from 4,268,000 in 1911 to 9,454,000 tons in 1920 while the total tonnage in 1913 was 5,312,000 tons. This is an increase in 9 years of more than 100%.

That an increase of 10% per year is not unreasonable to expect is evident from this. In that case the total foreign trade of the United States should reach in 11 years the 30 billion dollar mark.

The question arises, granting that New Orleans does handle 16 billion dollars foreign trade, how much do the other ports handle?

The foreign trade of New York in 1919 was 8 billion dollars, and of the other eastern ports, 2½ billions. The Pacific ports 1 billion, and the Gulf ports other than New Orleans 1 billion.

Now I believe that this is going to remain nearly the same for two reasons: first, there is no specific cause why the imports and exports of these harbors should especially increase above an average increase, and secondly, this average increase will be equal to the increase in dollar value, and if the exports and imports in dollars of these other ports is the same 10 years from now as it is today, they have in fact increased in tonnage to what I believe to be the extent of their natural increase.

If the total foreign trade of the United States did increase to 29½ billion dollars and if New Orleans secured from this 16 billion dollars, all other ports would handle 13½ billion or 8% more than what they now carry but because of the expected increase of dollar value, these harbors would see the tonnage of their foreign trade increase 47% in 15 years.

This 16 billion dollar trade of New Orleans and this 29½ billion dollar foreign trade of the United States will be, I estimate, divided as follows: (and I base my estimate on the condition of the other ports of the United States and the country behind them) 12 billion to Latin-America, of which New Orleans is to get 8 billion: 12 billion to the Southern Hemisphere outside Latin-America of which New Orleans is to get 6 billion and 4 billions to the other parts of the world of which New Orleans is to get 2 billions.

If Rotterdam, with only part of Holland and the Ruhrort behind it can get 27 billion tons in competition with such ports as Hamburg, Bremen, and Antwerp, certainly, New Orleans, without such competition and with the Mississippi Valley behind it may set 16 billion dollars foreign trade as her share.

The domestic trade multiplied itself 9 times in 25 years and yet all factories are working far below capacity today. That is because the export and import trade has fallen off, even more than is fully apparent because in dollar values it seems that our foreign trade and our domestic trade is more than it really is in tonnage.

Now for that reason I think the capacity for immediate increase in trade is available. I mean by this that if our foreign trade increases in such manner as I have above indicated, the factory output limitations are not going to be any drag on such growth, which is an important factor, as any heavy demand of foreign commerce will not immediately produce additional productive capacity.

The foreign trade of New Orleans of 1 billion dollars amounts now to 7 million tons. A 16 billion dollar trade through New Orleans will amount not to 112 million tons, but to 150 million tons on account of the increased value of the dollar, and only the Industrial Canal and Inner harbor can prepare New Orleans for such volume of business.

THE PORT FACILITIES OF NEW ORLEANS

The foregoing chapters showed how in the future the trade of half our country will move with increasing impetus in a northerly and southerly direction, and how it is possible, even seems probable, that in fifteen years from now, on account of this, the trade of New Orleans shall amount to from ten to fifteen-fold its present volume, or between 100 to 150 million tons per year.

Let us now see what facilities the port of New Orleans has to take care of such tonnage, and under what conditions the freight is now moving through this gateway.

TRANSPORTATION LINES

Ports in competing for trade must consider various controlling factors: in the first place, the cost of transportation. The second fundamental principle is, that with equal facilities for handling and equal costs of handling, the port with the widest choice of transportation facilities to or from the interior will be the most used port. In realization of the last principle, New Orleans has little to be wished for.

Of all Gulf ports, New Orleans is the only one that has, with such splendid system of feeding railroads, the in-and-outbound water service it can offer to shippers. Its connecting system of transportation lines is superb. This system has no inherent faults, nor do I know of any that could impede or work against a quick efficient and harmonious expansion, and it does possess all that is necessary for such expansion. It is New Orleans' saving grace and it counts for much. And as soon as the railroads have all learned (and the class is making rapid progress) that there is no case of waterways **versus** railways, but that it is waterways **and** railways, an important, nay, an all-important step is taken to make the attraction of New Orleans as a shipping center irresistibly alluring.

Five of the six trunk lines serving New Orleans are strong, of national prominence, and fan-like radiating from New Orleans, reach to the very marrow of America's backbone of foreign trade.

The Louisville and Nashville Railroad with her Mobile and Cincinnati terminals serves the east and northeast, between which

falls the Southern Railway with her Washington terminal. The Illinois Central Railroad runs due north to her Chicago and St. Louis terminal, evenly dividing the eastern lines from their western sisters.

The Southern Pacific connects, running almost due west, the Pacific coast and New Orleans, having to the south of her the Gulf Coast Lines to Brownsville and to the north the Texas and Pacific.

This splendid symphony of trunk lines is supplemented by four minor roads reaching as smaller arteries to the remotest corners of Louisiana. All combined offer a system in which each finds sufficient competition to avoid the evils of monopoly and not enough to run into the wastefulness of duplication.

Every one of these trunk and secondary lines has to contend with direct water competition: the Louisville and Nashville to Mobile, the Illinois Central and Gulf Coast Lines for their entire length; the Louisville and Nashville meets water competition from New Orleans also at Birmingham and Decatur, Ala., Nashville Tenn., and at her terminals Evansville, Louisville and Cincinnati.

The Southern Railway faces such water competition at Tuscaloosa and Florence, Ala., and Memphis, Tenn.; the Texas and Pacific to Shreveport, La., and the Southern Pacific for the entire run to Houston and Galveston, meeting it also at the Pacific coast.

And when we have learned true economy in our transportation problems, we shall have learned to say that those roads are supported by the water lines. Supported, feebly so, yes, but daily increasingly stronger, thanks to the Government-nursed barge lines. It is fortunate that the Government barge line is guided by a capable traffic expert. When the various kinks of rates and railroad interchange problems by means of government resources and this rate expert's ability have been worked out, it is time enough to look to some one that knows something about boats and rivers and canals and water transportation to guide the business and economical destinies of these barge lines.

A splendid tribute to the successful operation of the barge line can be seen in the recent determination of such an important railroad as the Illinois Central to cooperate with the barge line and to create a transfer for interchange of freight at Cairo, which means that freight carried from Cairo to New Orleans, or vice

38

versa, is accepted there through a joint traffic arrangement of a rail and water proportion. In other words, what would have been entirely carried by the Illinois Central Railroad alone, is now carried for the longer distance by water and the balance by the same road. The President of that Railroad pledged his readiness to participate in every reasonable (from his point of view) arrangement that may be suggested for the establishment of through rates and through routes. He too feels now that the interest of the country is poorly served if rail and water are antagonistic, each seeking to dominate a field that belongs to both of them, and now further admits that it will be better for the two to work in harmony.

I trust that since the ice is broken other rail lines will fall in line and accept water service as an aid in handling our commerce.

Railroads entering a harbor as terminus should have direct connections with the water edge of the port, or have a public organization giving them free and equal access to all vessels. It is generally believed that we have such an organization in the Public Belt Railroad and Dock Board.

However, there are four railroads that over their own lines and wharves reach shipside. They have a decided advantage over the other roads. These roads are the Southern with the old Frisco slips and Chalmette terminal, the Illinois Central with Stuyvesant Dock, the Texas and Pacific with Westwego, and the Southern Pacific with its Algiers docks, while the Louisville and Nashville is directly in contact with the Dock Board wharves.

The other roads must use the municipal Public Belt and the wharves controlled by the state Dock Board — two legs for one body, not always walking in the same direction.

I believe the governing bodies of these so greatly interdependent and interchanging limbs of our harbor, have met each other and know of each other. The railroads that must contend with this situation have remained small and can best be called secondary lines. They are the Gulf Coast Lines, Louisiana Railway and Navigation Company, New Orleans and Lower Coast line, and the Louisiana Southern. The remaining roads have been absorbed by the larger trunk lines having direct river access. But even these four trunk lines have far from a free hand in developing their river connections. Such development is checked , by the fear of Damocles' sword ever brandished by the Dock

Board who lets them never forget that they are there by sufferance of said Dock Board and not master of their wharves.

The Dock Board and its wharves, especially the Cotton Warehouse, are in turn handicapped by the independence of the Dock Board's chief rail feeder — the Municipal Public Belt Railway. Said wharves and warehouse are in no manner connected with the Public Belt beyond physical connections; two dogs with their hind legs bound together best illustrate such physical connection. The Cotton Warehouse is especially subjected to criticism and blame for the decline in our cotton trade, and while it has contributed to this decline, and other agencies have in no small degree caused this, yet some of the Cotton Warehouse's difficulties find their source in the fact that: the private railroads have their own terminals, the Public Belt not; the private terminals have their own railroads, the public wharves, not.

To better understand this problem and the solution offered, I shall first describe the Dock Board and the Public Belt.

THE DOCK BOARD

On the assumption that, contrary to illustrious examples of foreign countries (as for instance that of the London Port Authorities) we cannot find in New Orleans men in the shipping business sufficiently honest and public spirited to serve their community free from any motive of private gain, the appointed members of the Dock Board have always lacked sufficient experience in shipping matters or any intimate knowledge of what a harbor such as New Orleans is, really requires.

The fact that every Dock Board thought it necessary to actually run and operate our harbor as if they were hired experts always made such heavy demands upon their time that few men of business acumen measuring up to the great ability required by the harbor of New Orleans have been found willing to serve on this Dock Board.

These two reasons have made it extremely difficult to secure the proper personnel for the Dock Board even if the Governor of the State, in appointing these men, were always willing to turn a deaf ear to political motives coming from himself or his practical political friends, for although I feel that, notwithstanding opinions of the Louisiana Supreme Court and many others to the contrary, our Dock Boards have in the main not acted as political bodies,

40

yet it must be admitted that in minor matters such as rewarding jobs the Dock Board always did have a political value. Of course, exceptions here too prove the rule, and I have in mind how one governor many years ago removed the entire Dock Board to replace them with **his** supporters. So that members that are the right men doing the right thing, facing a particularly ungrateful task, rarely praised, might be recalled by any governor who values political work above the welfare of the harbor of New Orleans.

And so it was that we have had in our Dock Board a preponderous amount of absolutely unfit personnel who, often selected for want of better, felt themselves with their appointments cloaked overnight with the mantle of expert knowledge warranting them to run the destinies of this great gateway in the minutest detail. It is our great fortune (or misfortune?) that these men have invariably proven honest and anxious to serve well, but it must be greatly regretted that their smallness of mind and zeal to serve blinded them to the fact that they were unfit and incapable. However, had they been dishonest it might have been a blessing in disguise, calling thus forcibly attention to a great error in our harbor control.

We now have the two necessary means to forever avoid these serious difficulties. Under our new constitution we have provision for an over-lapping Dock Board and with the good will of our well-meaning governor who, alas, it not quite aware of the magnitude of his decision in this matter, but seems fully intent to do the right thing as he sees it, we may succeed in greatly eliminating any political drag upon future Dock Boards. But the greatest difficulty is going to be eliminated by having the new Dock Board functioning as a board of directors through a competent general manager, all-powerful, only owing obedience and responsibility to the Dock Board.

Let the Dock Board be made up of the highest type of citizens chosen from those that must use the harbor, men that would be selected as directors in a forty million dollar enterprise, as our harbor is. Let us not be afraid to appoint direct users of our harbors. We surely can find in this community honorable men that will sit on this Board and not take personal advantage over their competitors. But if this were not so, and if they were not restrained by public opinion, then there too, the general manager will be the solution, as he will execute a general policy laid down

by the Dock Board and be himself responsible for the operations and organization. Let the Dock Board meet as a Board of Directors once or twice a month, certainly not oftener, to outline a general policy within which the scope of the general manager has free play and full charge. Such man should be one that can command a salary of $40,000 or more, one that can operate the largest agency in the State, and in which lies the greatest interest of the State.

PUBLIC BELT

Most of the freight the Dock Board must receive or turn over to the Public Belt with which it has nothing in common beyond the supposed thought of each to work for the common good, one understanding this to mean the people of the State and let us hope beyond, the other the citizens of New Orleans.

The Public Belt has perhaps been sensitive to some political influence, but to all practical purposes it has been free from such.

The functioning of the Public Belt governing body has been so much more successful than that of the Dock Board that it may well make us pause and consider its composition: The Mayor as ex-officio chairman heads a Board of sixteen members. The sixteen members serve on overlapping terms for a sixteen year period, which is too long. They are appointed by the mayor. In the case of eleven of the sixteen, this appointing is only a confirmation and legalization of selections made by six business organizations. It meets twice a month and acts through a general manager who, urged on by an intent of purpose, has, through a generation's length of service given constancy of policy to the Public Belt.

Yet, perhaps due to the original amateurishness of these leaders, or the manner in which the Public Belt had to lift itself by the boot-straps, the Public Belt has drifted into a number of serious errors which already have done much harm, but which have not yet so ingrown but that an early correction can still efface every evil trace of them.

Commenced from nothing, developed from a shoestring, it was human for the leaders to gradually accept, as their handiwork and organization grew in importance, their views and opinions in the matter as self-sufficient. And as a natural result of this again their vision narrowed down as years passed on; their chariot

42

is far from hitched to a star, but very much to local immovable rails and switches, and they have untaught themselves to look far beyond local present-day issues into the bright and vast expanse of New Orleans' future. No broad general policy has been adopted so that we are still trying to pour the freight in and out of New Orleans through this narrow, kinky ribbon-like trench running between the city and its harbor, resulting in: (a) limiting the freight feeding to the river front to the capacity of the two ends of this long corridor; (b) an ever-increasing interference with street traffic and drays; (c) an ever-increasing demand for shed space; (d) an ever decreasing dispatch of vessels through the slowing down of our feeding over this increasingly more clogged ribbon of Belt Railway; (e) a blocking of further growth in capacity as soon as a certain point shall be reached not far distant. With three-fold the present car movement on the Public Belt the wharves would be continually shut from the city, forming an impassable barrier to drays and other street traffic, while the continuation of the Dock Board's and Public Belt's policy of extension along the river, punishing the city by spreading New Orleans' harbor front over a greater area, would only increase the demand upon the capacity of the ribbon at either end, and force the maintenance of tracks through radiating streets to and from the river front to relieve to some extent the ribbon's load. And with such spread out harbor front we would have made the same errors as most of the other American harbors, of which New York is today a notorious example. The entire harbor front mileages of Amsterdam, Antwerp, Bremen, Hamburg, Liverpool, London and Rotterdam added together is less than that of New York, although these cities handle six times New York's tonnage. Other results of this lack of broad policy and larger goal, not to say short-sightedness although better deserved, can be found in the aloofness from the Dock Board, the present state of our ferries, the absence of lighterage system, the chaos of our passenger and freight terminals tracks and yards, condition of our marginal street, and the unmethodical development as evident in a present pursuit of a bridge project.

Not the least of reasons for criticism can be found in the gradual acceptance of the policy that the development of the Public Belt must come out of its earning power.

The prime duty of such public body is first and all the time to serve and lead, not to be driven and pushed. It must anticipate wants, not wait until the fulfillment of wants becomes imperative. And such policy is unavoidable with the policy of growth on profits which latter policy has in itself another serious fault—it is misleading. It is leaning upon the commerce of our harbor and not lifting this commerce, but is pushed onward by the pressure of business; it does not break and lead the way, but our commerce must push it forward while breaking a way for itself. The entire Public Belt property now representing a value of $2,200,000 has found its base on the profits of the service rendered, and the extent of its growth seems to be limited to the amount of profits it can make in serving the harbor. It earned last year after paying all interest charges $116,000 or 14½% on a equity of $800,000 grown from a cash investment of $200,000.

The Public Belt is facing from time to time some general criticism, some shippers attaching to it the odium of politics, a few railroad "officials" inefficiency in operation, unreliability and high-handedness in settling claims, but I am convinced that any impartial and competent investigation of these charges will quickly show the importance of these claims magnified through bias.

The Public Belt feels itself handicapped through delays in installing proper facilities, switches and trackage caused by the Dock Board, and lack of cooperation of the private shippers in promptly unloading the cars.

The shippers state that with the present limited track facilities they cannot secure a sufficient unincumbered flow of freight over the Public Belt Railroad to and from the wharves sufficiently fast to keep up with the speed of loading or unloading the vessel.

The goal of the Public Belt Railroad should be set clearly and definitely without further delay by a commission made up of the general manager of the Public Belt, an expert and a man appointed by the railroads entering New Orleans, and towards such a goal the policy of the Public Belt should be fixed.

It should stop just growing but aspire to attain.

I believe such commission must make the following recommendation:

(I) The acquisition of all the trackage and terminals, both passenger and freight within the parish of New Orleans, and in some cases as far outside of the Parish as seems expedient and

44

can be agreed upon with the railroad involved. This can have as results:

(a) The change of status of the Public Belt from a switching road to a trunk line, with the therewith going tariff changes and carriers' charges (absorptions and unloading by Belt). This would solve the great problem of interchange of freight between the railroads entering New Orleans and the Public Belt line, and the cotton warehouse, grain elevator, coal tipple and wharves.

It should also end the lack of coordination- between the rail facilities in New Orleans and mean:

(b) The ultimate removal of all railroad tracks from the city streets, except those along the river front, the Public Belt connecting with the Southen Pacific, Texas and Pacific, Gulf Coast Line, Yazoo and Mississippi Valley Railroad, Illinois Central Railroad, and Louisiana Railway and Navigation Company at Southport and to the north thereof, and across the Industrial Canal with the Southern Railway, Louisville and Nashville, and Louisiana Southern Railway.

(c) One Union Passenger Depot to be built north of the Fair Grounds where practically a direct connection with all the railroads entering New Orleans can be made; Gentilly, Esplanade, Claiborne, Rampart, Carrollton, City Park Avenue and Jefferson Davis Parkway giving splendid street connections.

(d) For each road a freight yard interchange just within the parish limits, in addition to this one passenger train yard to be located north of the Fair Grounds between Bayou St. John and Rosehill Cemetery.

(e) The Dock Board to own all the docks and wharves and their equipment.

(II) Car ferry incline to be built capable of docking four car ferries at one and the same time at: Southport, between Broadway and Audubon Park, immediately below the Cotton Warehouse at the cost of part of Stuyvesant Dock, at the foot of Terpsichore Street, and at the foot of Esplanade, giving street traffic a free and rarely encumbered entrance to the docks at Carrollton Avenue, State Street, Louisiana Avenue, Washington Avenue, Felicity Street, Julia Street, Canal Street, Conti Street, Dumaine Street, Press Street, and Louisa Street.

(III) A marginal street eighty feet in width skirting the river side of the Belt Railroad paralleling the docks — in that manner relieving street traffic and dray movement from the wharves.

45

(IV) Use of the present Louisiana Railway and Navigation Company tracks as freight line for local merchandise shipped or delivered in L. C. L.

(V) The postponement of present bridge plans to be replaced by a substantial car floatage system by means of car ferries of 32-car capacity.

(VI) A lighterage system permitting the loading and unloading of vessels from river side.

(VII) The changing of the present rail dock connection to the individual switch saw tooth system, in that manner increasing the available dock space 100% and increasing the dispatch 250 to 300%.

(VIII) The complete control over all trolley car system and power houses.

(IX) The ultimate electrification of all railroads within the parish.

(X) Full control of all ferry service supplemented with a passenger service on the river, canal, lake and Bayou St. John, connecting the passenger station, the Industrial Canal and all river points and docks with an efficient and quick service.

While it should be understood that many of the provisions look far into the future, some such plan should be adopted and placed as goal to work to for these reasons:

(a) It is the most efficient transportation arrangement, and nothing should be permitted to arise to impede or block this ultimate goal.

(b) It contains many provisions that can immediately be placed in effect and that will greatly increase the efficiency of our port.

(c) It reduces considerably the handling charges and increases the dispatch of vessels.

(d) It places all transportation facilities under one control and avoids expensive duplication of service.

(e) The moment is not for distant that any further increase of freight through our port will make it impractical to handle it with the present situation.

The money can be found through a blanket bond issue guaranteed by the City on all property thus involved; the railroads, railways and ferries.

The assessed value of the property involved is fifty-two million dollars; the present revenue of these facilities is $7,900,000. In ten years the entire property could be owned by the city free of any charge or lien—and the cost of operating could be substantially reduced.

COMBINATION OF DOCK BOARD AND PUBLIC BELT

The Public Belt and the Dock Board are interdependent parts of one body, in the harmonious operation of which parts we, the body, are vitally interested.

In view of this truth and former statements regarding the Dock Board and the Public Belt, I suggest that.

FIRST: The Dock Board be made up as follows:

One man suggested to the Governor by the Association of Commerce.

One man suggested to the Governor by the New Orleans Board of Trade.

One man suggested to the Governor by the New Orleans Steamship Operators.

One man selected by the Governor from other harbor interests.

One man selected by the Governor from the Public Belt.

SECOND: The Public Belt and the Dock Board to meet in one supreme body consisting of the Governor as chairman, the Mayor, and the President of the Dock Board, to be called into session by the Governor or Dock Board or Public Belt Commission.

THIRD: The authority of the Dock Board to be confined to all immovable river front and warehouse property and mechanical loading and unloading devices and wharf equipment; the Public Belt to all transportation facilities such as railroads, trolley cars, lighterages, ferries, freight yards, passenger depots, freight depots and in addition the power plants.

This gives the advantage of absolute public control and ownership of all river front property—properly balanced and coordination of authority.

THE WHARVES AND SHEDS

The total length of New Orleans wharves under Dock Board control is about five and a half miles, of which four miles are provided with sheds. These wharves are in peak load very, and under usual conditions fairly congested; yet they had passed over them only 5,137,901 tons (1920), or about 170 tons per year per lineal foot, or about one-half a ton per day, a very low average.

47

However, if the wharves were properly used, built and equipped, there would have been no reason why we could not surpass or at least equal the performance of most European ports that carry three to five tons, or six to nine times the tonnage per lineal foot that we do, across their wharves.

Yet our wharves are considered so congested that the present Dock Board felt warranted in even trying to use the foot of Canal Street for additional shed space.

The wharves were built a generation ago and show no improvements in that period. They are inefficient for many reasons. But inefficient as they are we use them only to 50% of their capacity, through total lack of lighterage.

Some of the serious objections that can be raised against the present wharves are the following:

When a ship makes port, it must discharge its cargo as rapidly as possible and cannot wait with this unloading to allow the cargo to be taken away. The cargo must also be spread out to afford opportunity to sort it according to marks and consignees. Likewise in loading.

The stevedores can work rapidly and load correctly only when the cargo can be loaded and stowed in the proper sequence, which means that freight must be available in the order wanted. For this purpose as much of the heavy freight as possible should be on the wharf prior to the arrival of the vessel, and the balance must be held in railroad cars at the risk of demurrage, tying up equipment, and blocking the railroad tracks. Of course in a less busy season the freight can be placed on wharves not otherwise occupied. But this is at cost of additional dockage, wharfage and sheddage charges and necessitates the movement of freight, or the moving of ships from one wharf to another, a costly and unsatisfactory affair.

The usual way to avoid congestion and shed demurrage is for the steamship line not to order the freight out, and if this is not convenient, the shipper may use another port.

(I) The wharves give no evidence of sufficient consideration to the possible nature of the freight movement which the wharf must mediate.

The true basis of wharf construction is the determination of such movement and above all upon the equipment which will be put upon it.

48

(II) The sheds' construction does not allow the installation of tiering machines such as telphers, monorail, etc. Yet such tiering is very necessary to economy.

Where mechanical tiering is not possible through lack of equipment as is the case on our river front, cargo should have space enough without the need of piling it more than shoulder high.

It is more economical to hand-truck 400 feet than lift 10 feet by man power. However, by mechanical tiering, freight can be tiered 30 feet with little, if any additional expense over tiering 5 feet by man power.

Assuming an average height of tiering at 15 ft. a shed can hold about thrice the cargo held with hand tiering, taking into consideration distributing space. At a tiering height of 15 ft. a shed of 60 ft. width and 500 ft. length has a capacity of 6000 tons at 70 cubic ft. per ton with ample distributing space left. Now we require for this, sheds of 190 to 200 ft. width with subsequent greater maintenance and stevedoring cost.

With lighterage and mechanical stevedoring equipment, and with saw-tooth-land-side shed and individual car spotting track, 400 ft. length of shed would easly suffice for a 6000 ton ship (even permitting one-sixth of the ships cargo to be tiered not higher than 5 ft. it being general cargo and not fit for high tiering) about equal the wharf length the ship with its clearance would occupy, and still be able to receive and deliver cargo as fast as the ship will permit, which is about eight times as fast as now is possible over our shedded wharves.

(III) There is no harmony between the capacity of the wharves, sheds, rail and streets.

(IV) The sheds are too wide. If the width of the sheds can be kept within the above limits of 60 ft. the cost of the sheds will be less than is usual now, as there will be only one short span, and besides no posts will interfere with the freight movement. The width of sheds is also of course costly in trucking the freight from car to ship, and although the railroads absorb the unloading costs and really are obligated to bring the freight within reach of the ship's tackle, they rarely do this, but unload it and bring it in the sheds. They absorb these costs except on local freight that is not competitive freight, where they make a charge varying with the commodity. New Orleans is of course more interested in the local than in the through freight.

49

(V) The wharves are not sufficiently supported by an efficient marginal street and paved approach streets, giving, however, a passage for drays in the center of the wharf, so that most drays and all where possible seek this wharf passage, increasing the length of passage of freight from the railroad car to the steamship, decreasing storage capacity of all the wharves, increasing risk of pilferage, increasing risk of damage, which anyone will appreciate if he sees a four-mule drawn dray flying through such sheds.

(VI) Further criticism can be made of the floors which do not permit efficient trucking over the wharves, be it power or hand driven.

(VII) The lighting system is faulty and leaves much to be wished for.

(VIII) The opportunity for pilferage is far too great.

(IX) The wharves are practically devoid of any mechanical devices for carrying freight over the sheds into the steamer or railroad cars, or vice versa.

(X) They are far from rat-proof, and all rat-proof regulations so rigidly enforced in 1914 have been greatly slackened.

(XI) The rail connections with the wharves are wrong, forcing the spotting of cars in train formation instead of the individual car movement, which would increase the car space alone 50 %.

(XII) Through the inefficiency of these wharves we have a congested river front which makes it difficult to assign regular wharves to steamship lines. The accumulation of cargo is in this manner very expensive and slow.

A proper shipping necessity is that established lines have assigned to them regular wharves, subject to their sole use.

(XIII) Not any accommodations ever brightened the life of any human being on our river front.

Unknown are comfort stations to passengers and workmen alike; telegraph and telephone booths are conspicuous through their absence, no coffee-house or lunch-room ever profaned the Dock Board's wharves. We need a modern, simple but comfortable restaurant on our river front for visitors and a series of high grade sanitary lunch rooms for our workmen.

Yet the public should be segregated from the wharves proper, perhaps by means of a balcony or otherwise so that the public could freely inspect and visit but not come in actual interference with the freight.

CRANES AND MECHANICAL WHARF EQUIPMENT

There are four distinct groups of mechanical devices needed on the wharf: ship loading and unloading equipment, shed cargo handling, tiering, and dray or car loading and unloading. New Orleans has some ship unloading and loading mechanical equipment, a large part of which is in private hands.

The private control of our hoisting apparatus is a severe handicap. The charges are prohibitive and other conditions pertaining to their use make such use pratically impossible.

At the present time there is no switch track available for the general use of the private floating cranes, as the switches now connecting direct with wharves where shipment can be handled by a derrick boat, are under control of different shipping interests. Too much red tape and approvals are required in the use of the cranes.

The Dock Board does own 14 banana conveyors, 7 conveyors at the Bienville wharf, 5 at the Southern Pacific, and one portable conveyor made up of four sections. There are a number of private locomotive cranes, six private floating derricks and five private stationary derricks, but outside of this Dock Board and private equipment New Orleans depends chiefly upon the ship's tackle, like Central American ports. It misses the most economical and efficient transfer machinery, the gantry crane.

Marseille, France, handles 221 tons per lineal wharf foot including the unequipped front, but 563 tons over the crane-equipped part, 250% more. Marseille operates 612 cranes. Sometimes eight to ten cranes work one ship.

To load and unload a general cargo from a 9,000 ton vessel by means of mechanical appliances in two days should be a possible average goal for New Orleans.

It is by such machinery as is installed in ports in England, Germany, France, Holland, Belgium, Argentine or Brazil that 6 or 9 thousand tons transference per day are to be compared with a 1,500 ton record at New Orleans.

The ship's detention will be one-fourth to one-sixth the time, and for the same docks four times as many ships can be berthed in a given period. And the overhead charges would be also one-fourth. The above figures refer to miscellaneous cargoes.

The cost of discharging and loading the vessel and the cost of cargo handling, which may include assorting as well as distribu-

ting and tiering, should with proper mechanical equipment not be over 40ȼ per ton with present day labor costs. Two cranes usually work at each hatch. The minimum speed of discharge should be 60 tons of general cargo per crane hour.

Cranes should be spaced not more than 90 feet and movable along the river front, thus New Orleans should have about 320 gantry wharf cranes. We have none. Antwerp has 430 cranes.

The movements in the shed consist in receiving to or delivery from ships, trucks, drays, cars, lighters and in checking, sorting, distributing and tiering.

Useful in such work are the electric trucks with trailers and skids, telpher or monorail trolley, portable conveyor. We have some electric trucks and one portable conveyor.

It may on general terms be said: Our river front is devoid of much needed mechanical equipment.

STEVEDORING COST

The stock in trade of the stevedoring firm is its labor control. In New Orleans such control is either not efficient enough, or through mistaken self-interest it permitted labor to block the installation of modern mechanical labor saving devices in the loading and unloading of vessels. And except where this was done, through the elimination of the stevedore or through the power of the shipping interest involved as for instance the banana conveyors of the Fruit Company or the inclined elevators of the Southern Pacific, and also excepting a few conveyors, there has been no modern device installed on New Orleans river front, and none of the smaller shipping interests has proven strong enough to over-ride such labor opposition, nor has the Dock Board been able to do so. Yet often has the New Orleans stevedore proven strong enough to secure wharf space where the ship agent failed. And it is thus true to say: the New Orleans stevedoring firm's stock in trade is not labor control but political influence which does not leave them free to go counter to labor's maxims.

As a direct result of this we must also accept the high stevedoring rates which figure at an average of $1.30 per ton for loading and $1.10 per ton for unloading, which permits the payment of the highest wages in New Orleans.

That this has been possible is chiefly due to the small number of independent stevedoring firms.

In some cases there is a baser, more nefarious reason. It is where the ship's agents do not care to see the stevedoring charges reduced, being themselves interested in the stevedoring firms, and in that manner participate in the rake-off and extra profit not accounted for in their bills to the foreign ship operator.

Some of the charges all reduced to the ton of 40 cubic feet as unit follow: Loading aluminum dust $2; steel plates $1.50, over 33 feet length $2; rail $1.40; creosoted lumber $2; screwed cotton $2.40, hand stowed $1.32; tobacco $3; barrel goods $1.20; miscellaneous $1.40.

Unloading: coffee $1.20; pyrites $1; logs $1.25; phosphates $1.10; ballast $1.30; bricks $1.50; refined sugar $1.20.

Yet it would be possible to even keep these wages on the present level regardless of the increasing dollar's value, and at the same time reduce the cost of stevedoring per ton to half the present cost were the modern mechanical aids installed. There are two other ways of reducing the labor cost without cutting in the effective pay of the laborer.

The uncertainty of employment and large amount of enforced idleness and payment of certain rake-offs 'cause the laborer to receive in the long run not too large a wage.

Let either the Dock Board employ all stevedoring labor, in that manner keeping the supply more nearly to the demand and lessen the percentage of idleness or let all such labor be classified as either permanent or extra labor. The permanent receiving a constant weekly income but figured at a smaller unit per hour; the extra not receiving a fixed income, but a larger unit per hour of actual work.

Perhaps the combination of all three remedies would be the best. That is, let the Dock Board do all the stevedoring under a fixed charge of say half the present prevailing prices, install all modern mechanical aids, employ a fixed number of men at fixed wages plus bonus, and create a surplus reserve of extra men paid higher hourly wages when employed.

DRAYAGE

A source of great expense in New Orleans is the costly drayage; costly on account of three reasons:

(I) The necessity of serving a large area with unnecessarily greatly scattered terminals, warehouses and factories.

(II) Poor condition of streets and pavements. If all the streets at the rear of and parallel to the docks were paved they would relieve the great congestion of the few paved streets now serving the docks. Some of the so-called paved streets are in such condition that economical passage is impossible, and there where they are fairly decent, the approach to the wharves is poor.

(III) The Public Belt and other switching between wharves and streets delay the drays greatly. But even taking these three reasons into consideration, still the dray rates are high. Charges run from $1.28 to $1.48 per ton for cotton, $1.20 per ton for coffee. For that money it could be loaded and carried 250 miles by water. The best way to eliminate these drayage charges is to make drayage unnecessary or as nearly unnecessary as possible, and by having the Public Belt make a store door delivery and thus inaugurate a dray system of its own—soon to do all the draying alone in New Orleans.

WAREHOUSES

The most important harbor facility to the city itself is the warehouses. It is the warehouse that brings local benefits and business opportunities. With it the city may retain some of the freight passing through it, give rise to local brokerage firms, markets of deposits and finally industries.

Economy, abundance and efficiency in warehouse space is needed to a harbor city as a good digestion to an individual. New Orleans is particularly backward in this respect. The required storage and warehouse space for New Orleans is right now 70 million square feet, of which we have only 3½ million, not taking into account the Army Supply Base for obvious reasons given further. With proper warehouse facilities New Orleans should be a market of deposit for coffee, sugar, sisal, rice, cotton, grain, fruit, meat, steel, sulphur, salt, rosin, turpentine, rubber, spices, tobacco, hides, jute, tin and many others. We get along without such warehouses as a day laborer gets along without college training. He doesn't need it in his work; we don't need it now. He could not be a day laborer with it, would find use for it if he had it. We could not be merely a transit harbor and would find use for the warehouses if we had them.

Mannheim (Baden) has 150 warehouses. 25 of these are exclusively devoted to tobacco, 10 to grain, 23 to coffee, etc.

A great essential for economy in warehouse operation is its location, which should be such as to be served by the maximum rail and water lines and streets, and it should be centrally located.

The duties of a warehouse are the following three:

(I) To receive and deliver at an absolute minimum cost and time delay, the goods stored.

(II) To store them safely and cheaply without deterioration.

(III) To classify and vouch for through negotiable receipt for the quality and quantity of the goods stored.

None of the warehouses in New Orleans responds to all these three duties combined; some of them respond to none of these duties.

The latest, the Army Supply Base, is not economically accessible to drays and its elevators are located inside instead of outside the building, while the rear buildings can only be used in connection with the river at prohibitive cost. The rear buildings might as well have been located in the interior of the city on the Public Belt for the good they do shipping from water connection. Yet such water connection was in mind in its location, otherwise it would not have been placed on the water's edge. In this manner by far the larger part of the Army Supply Base can be served by Public Belt Railroad alone.

An efficient warehouse system is a step towards local industrial development. It commences with slight local improvements to the goods stored, and leads to complete altering its shape and composition. The compresses, cooperage, barrelling, sawmills, are some of such first steps. We are practically without such facilities or they are so poorly placed that they lose much of their efficiency.

Bonded warehouses are practically unknown in New Orleans, while cold storage warehouses are few and poorly located.

THE COTTON WAREHOUSE

There is one public warehouse in New Orleans and this is the well-known Cotton Warehouse — built of reinforced concrete in 1914 at a cost of six million dollars, with the idea of giving loading space to five ships at one time. This has so far not materialized. Its fullest capacity of 320,000 bales was almost reached once, and its business has been declining ever since, although the cotton trade of Galveston grew. Its average load last year and the year before last was 55%.

55

The loading capacity of the warehouse into ships is 7,500 bales per **day.** It loaded last **year** 143,705 bales into ships.

It can handle 3,000,000 bales of incoming cotton per year. It handled the year ending August 31, 1918, 23% of that capacity; 1919, 22%; 1920, 16%; and I predict that this year it will not do 12% of its capacity. Yet it made last month alone after paying the interest on its investment $24,342 profit.

In 1920 it still did 50% of New Orleans business, indications are so far this year that this figure will be 38¼%. The other twelve privately owned presses having less than one-half the storage capacity of the Cotton Warehouse handled about 20% less, yet these privately owned warehouses are obsolete — the Cotton Warehouse modern.

The cotton warehouse is inefficient because it is necessary to handle usually, ten, yes, sometimes 40 times the number of bales to reach one; its charges are too high; its organization arbitrary and not efficient; the cotton is subject to delays in delivering; unsatisfactory sampling and cost of loading add to the difficulties. As a result of all this we see that although in New Orleans' cotton territory more cotton is grown than in the hinterland of any other port, we handled last year less than half that which went through Galveston, and while New Orleans lost 22% of her cotton trade, Galveston increased hers 35%.

This decrease was again most marked in the Cotton Warehouse which was 50% greater than that of the private warehouses. Fifteen cotton firms in business today in New Orleans are pulling stakes and moving to other ports, chiefly to Galveston.

(I) The Cotton Warehouse's storage charges are too high, as may be deducted from the following. The warehouse is filled on an average, to 55% of its capacity although it is right now, due to stagnation in the business filled to 81%. In 1920 it received over $530,000 for storage alone. And since this does not include anything else but storage, as extra charges are made for receiving, checking, tagging, weighing, skidding, turning, splitting warehouse receipts, compressing, removing bands, furnishing missing ties, patching, sewing patches on, marking, cutting off spiders, delivery, demurrage, ranging, ordering out, charges, sampling, rejecting, yard service, applying tags furnished by owner—this storage revenue alone represents a charge of 9% on the cotton warehouse investment including presses, trackage, range yards, equipment, etc.

56

(II) The four trunk lines that have their own wharves certainly do not facilitate the movement of cotton via Public Belt and Public Cotton Warehouse, and the entire absence of any control over the Public Belt by the Cotton Warehouse or vice versa is certainly not advantageous to the Cotton Warehouse where on the other hand the private railroads control their own wharves.

(III) Distances throughout the cotton warehouse are very great, and export cotton cannot always come in on tracks adjacent to the wharves.

At Galveston, compresses are so close to where ships load that moving the cotton from the compresses suffices to put cotton to shipside at no more expense than would attend ordinary press operation.

(IV) In practice very few ships can come for general cargo to the cotton warehouse, but come for cotton alone, which means hauling of the ship about.

(V) The cost of handling the cotton through the cotton warehouse is entirely too high. A bale received, weighed, stowed a month and a day and delivered with range and yard service of one day must pay $1.59.

To this must be added drayage and stevedoring charges making a total of about $2.75 which does not include compressing or any of the other 31 possible charges.

The decline in our cotton business is of course not solely due to the above obstructions. Our foreign trade, the Texas rail rates, the passing of the local cotton factor have had their effects, but that does not explain why private warehouses suffer less. The cotton warehouse could greatly reduce its charges and make more money through greater volume of business and help this port in the manner it should.

PRIVATE WAREHOUSES

The private warehouses here in New Orleans are situated away from the wharves and only a few of them could by any stress of words be called modern, fire and rat-proof, on account of which the insurance and the damage to the goods stored and handled are not on the low level they should be.

On the other hand, the charges are held at too high a level.

They vary with the demand and are not always alike but the prevailing charges for storage are the lowest for the four principal commodities and are from 5 to 7¢ per 100 lbs. sack per month for flour, 12¢ per barrel for sugar, 8¢ per bag for coffee, and 5¢ per pocket for rice. In addition to this there is a handling charge of from 60¢ to $2 per ton and one mill per month insurance.

It need not cost more than $3.50 per square foot to build the most modern fully equipped fire-proof warehouse with rail and water connections and outside elevators.

Allowance must be made for an average yearly vacancy which under good business operation and management should not exceed a yearly revenue loss of 33%. This would mean that every two square feet must drum up a living for three, or every square foot must be charged with an investment of $5.25.

A fixed overhead for interest, depreciation, maintenance, taxes and insurance of 13¾% is fair and would mean an annual charge of 72¢ per square foot or 6¢ per square foot per month.

This would warrant for such modern warehouse a charge of 3½¢ per 100 lbs. sack for flour, 8¢ per barrel for sugar, 4¢ per bag for coffee, and 3¢ per pocket for rice, which figures include a profit of 2% per year, which profit may be substantially increased if the management succeeds in keeping the warehouse more nearly loaded to its capacity than I allowed. For instance, if the warehouse were the year around loaded to its capacity, an additional 8% profit on the investment could be shown.

As it is always desirable for a modern warehouse to have a very liquid storage, charges should be made per day, to be altered to a monthly charge after 27 days.

The average handling charge with modern equipment should not exceed $1 per ton (receiving and delivering) with $1 as minimum charge. To all of this one-half cent per unit per month for insurance, administration, weighing, certifying, and guaranteeing should be added.

The high and varying charges and the risk of the private warehouse have added their mighty influence against New Orleans becoming a market of deposit with industries growing on account of abundant supply of raw material.

It is a fact that sugar and rice are stored now at distant points because of insufficient facilities here and rates of storage which make the planter hold his product rather than store it at New

Orleans, thus saving the expense of storing it here rather than take advantage of New Orleans as a market of deposit.

The lack of public licensed warehouse space at New Orleans was largely responsible for the congestion on the docks last year.

It is then urged, by private gain alone, and that only from a short-sighted policy, that these private warehousemen so violently opposed turning the Army Supply Bases over to private use.

PUBLIC GRAIN ELEVATOR

New Orleans is blessed with one of the best operated, most modern grain elevators of the world, although an error of omission was committed when insufficient provisions for barge-grain were made, which error is now being corrected.

New Orleans owes a public debt to the man that so successfully planned and operated this splendid utility.

FUELING

There are at present no proper fueling facilities in New Orleans. Bunker coal is loaded in the slow, awkward, costly and dusty manner of derrick hoist and dump, permitting no satisfactory check upon the quantity delivered.

Many of these objections will be removed by the new coal tipple but it is against economy to force vessels to go under the coal tipple. Yet the first need now is bunkering facilities, only when coal is cargo can the use of this coal loading plant be desirable. However the plant now being built will find itself handicapped in its limited yard space, if used as cargo coal loading plant, nor is its location a fortunate one.

The only proper method is, as has been accepted in the larger harbors of Europe and South America, the 1,000-ton self-propelled barge fueling lighter which puts the coal into bunkers at low cost without dust at the rate of 500 tons an hour, or better, weighed accurately while pouring in, not interfering with lighters lying alongside the vessel, bringing the fuel to the vessel at her berth.

Harbor tank fuel lighters pumping the fuel oil into the bunker tanks of oil burners should in like manner be available.

PASSENGER ACCOMODATIONS

'This is an unknown facility in New Orleans for the passenger of ocean vessels or river boats alike. No attempt to facili-

tate his approach to or from the river has in any manner been made, and customhouse and immigration inspection is carried on under great difficulties on that account. As stated when describing the wharves, there are no lunch counters, telegraph or telephone booths and comfort stations on the wharves.

It is very difficult for the ordinary man, or stranger not traveling by auto, to reach our river front, and many wharves can only be reached after a considerable walk over poorly paved streets not passable to ladies after a reasonably heavy rainfall.

There is no other passenger service on our river than directly across it, the most of us owe our views of the river to occasionally visiting excursion boats. I consider the opportunity for the public to see the harbor a very essential one. An afternoon or evening spent under comfortable conditions on the river increases in a most needed way interest in our harbor.

We are sadly in need of first-class passenger service between various river points, and I regret that this service in New Orleans has been totally ignored. Even the ferries are obsolete, uncomfortable, filthy, dangerous and obscene; their landings are everything that a ferry landing should not be, and instead of being operated for public good, they are exploited and are operated for profits—just as fundamentally wrong as charging tolls on streets.

RIVER TERMINAL

Perhaps due to the absence of extensive river traffic, New Orleans lacks the necessary and proper river terminals and as a consequence of this we have an unreasonably high cost of loading and unloading of river vessels.

As New Orleans' very location is predicated upon the river, and as New Orleans' future position as a harbor will find its main support in real river service, efficient river terminals are greatly needed.

TOWING AND DRY-DOCKING

The harbor of New Orleans can justly be proud of its towing facilities, and although the towing charges cannot be called modest —yet they are not unfair and can favorably compare with those of other harbors.

Equally fortunate is our city with ample dry docking facilities that will undoubtedly expand as need warrants.

LIGHTERAGE

The practical entire absence of lighters in New Orleans is a very severe handicap and the cause of our missing a source of great economy.

The lighter largely alleviates the penalties of uncertain arrival of the vessel, demurrage, congestion, possible car shortage and lack of space on public wharves.

Without it we must load our vessels from one side alone, haul them frequently about, meet an expensive switching bill, and sacrifice a great deal of possible dispatch. The river should have a large fleet of lighters carrying the freight at 3^f per ton per day.

The lighter is a necessary tool in any harbor no matter how well the harbor may be equipped. The harbor lighter and the belt line fill each other out.

The lighter being more flexible, more cheaply moved about, and carrying more in one load, is more economical than any land carrier. A seven hundred-ton lighter is perhaps at present best for New Orleans. Such a lighter would cost about one-third the cost of similar capacity in rolling stock.

In some cases, the self-propelled lighter with its own loading and unloading equipment is preferable and such should be built of steel and would cost about as much as rolling stock of like capacity without the locomotive. Supporting these large train-load lighters, the harbor will find effective use for smaller 50 and 100-ton lighters. 63% of all freight unloaded from vessels in Hamburg prior to the war was received on barges or lighters. Rotterdam, and Amsterdam show even higher percentage of lighterage.

In New Orleans' case, lighterage would be particularly promising as ⅓ of the area of the parish and ⅛ of the state of Louisiana is water surface.

PROTECTION

Our harbor is lacking in fire and police boats, but a few more disastrous fires and victories of strikers' navy may arouse the ire öf the Dock Board and police to action.

For that purpose certain appointed Dock Board employees should have policing power.

SPECIAL BULK AND COMMODITY HARBORS

New Orleans lacks every vestige of bulk or commodity harbors. This is a very important oversight, slackness or blunder, the effects of which are marked and may long be felt. The lumber exports of Gulfport, the oil movement of the Sabine district and the cotton trade of Galveston are forcible proofs of what the result of such slackness may be. Had we built, for instance, a proper oil harbor nine or ten years ago, our oil industry would not have been so scattered, scatted and scathed. A proper oil harbor would either have been located across the river or at this side at the end of a pipe line. Such river oil pipe line could have been created without prohibitive expense through an oilproof canvas 20-inch hose specially made for that purpose; flat when laid across the river bottom, to be filled gradually after laying, in that manner never subjecting the "pipe" line to any hydraulic pressure without providing immediately an equalizing compensating counter interior pressure.

Such oil harbor would have held the ships in a current-free basin, completely segregated from the other part of the port, and given the fullest fire protection to the industries located on the shores of the basins, or those in its vicinity. With such proper arrangements New Orleans would now have been the largest oil harbor of the United States and the low fuel cost would have been an added inducement to vessels to call at New Orleans.

Such harbor would in addition to this have a favorable influence upon the insurance rates of most of our river industries.

What has been said about the oil harbor may be an echo regarding our lumber business. We have no facilities whatever for the accumulation and handling of lumber, no lumber cranes, pools, assorting and storage places where lumber would have been held available for prompt and economical delivery. We should be the market and storage place for lumber, with a storage capacity of 100 million feet (one firm alone held here in the summer of 1919 under these adverse conditions 20 million feet in private storage), where our own forest products would meet the lumber from South America and the Northwestern States. Now forced through sheer necessity and fighting for existence in this present day business struggle for life, some private interests are seriously considering making such investment and would have done so long ago had it not been for monoply of public ownership. Some such steps have

62

already been taken across the river and some day soon if we don't get busy quick we may again tell each other what might have been.

Steel interests have a similar story to tell, almost monotonous in its repetition. It costs now up to $2.40 per ton to load steel plates and due to abuse received in handling, the plates often arrive at destination in such damaged condition that urgent requests reach the shipper to kindly avoid repetition of this even at the cost of selecting another port. Had it not been for these facts New Orleans would have been long ago the port for Gary, Chicago and Birmingham.

Heavy machinery and boilers shipment at a crane hire of from $200 to $300 per day with a minimum of $75 for any job seems well nigh impossible through our "efficient and splendidly equipped harbor with its magnificent facilities".

Almost every other bulk movement has a story of its own, and for what New Orleans is today we must pay homage to our location which pulled us through regardless of our own drag.

HARBOR FINANCES

In spite of the marine strike the net earnings of the Dock Board during May, 1921, were $23,593.74 greater than May, 1920. The gross revenues from all sources for the month totalled $310,556.50, of which about half was for operating expense, one-sixth for interest on investment (bonds) leaving 33% as extra profits, or 16% on the investment. The cotton warehouse showed a net profit for the month of $24,342.46—"As the entire plant is public property, revenues will be only such as are necessary to cover cost of operation, interest charges upon a 5% bond issue, a sinking fund to retire the bonds, and a small reserve for contingencies"—(Quotation from tariff sheet published by the Dock Board.)

The gain over the previous and all other fiscal years continue. Since September 1, 1920, until May 31, 1921, the net profit of all departments has been $1,165,271.36, as compared to $364,987, for the corresponding nine months a year ago. Surely a splendid money making enterprise.

Since it is evidently impossible to tax all our freight away we could gouge perhaps more golden eggs from our harbor users. We have apparently not yet surpassed the limit of what the traffic can bear.

63

The grain elevator showed a profit from September 1, 1920‘
to Arpil 30, 1921, of $141,418.25. The net earnings for the
same period for the cotton warehouse are $92,701.19.

Of these total earnings $545,913.23 were spent in dock im-
provements, $50,257.39 in additional fire protection for the Cot-
ton Warehouse, $57,364.45 for extensions at the grain elevator.
Other covered profits are found in the fire and liability plan.
The fire fund started ten years ago contains $490,000 after the
$120,000 to cover the loss of the Desire Street wharf last Novem-
ber has been deducted. The employers liability fund started
three years ago has grown to $312,491.43. The explanation is
easy:

"The board may issue bonds to an amount the annual interest
upon which is not in excess of the average net revenue for the
two fiscal years immediately preceding."—La. Constitution.

It is thus evident that one industry is taxed for the creation
of facilities for another, often overburdening such first industry.
Cotton must pay for a possible lumber harbor, etc.

The total gross revenue of the Dock Board was in 1920:

DOCKS AND WHARVES:

Dockage	$816,057.31
Sheddage	150,351.70
License	4,227.00
Harbor dues	28,422.50
Mechanical devices	70,645.78
Tollage	177,679.98
"First Call"	72,536.45
Rentals	25,813.08
Miscellaneous	12,449.00
	$1,365,212.80
Cotton Warehouse	1,313,694.38
Grain Elevator	506,984.07

Total gross revenue for 1920 ____ $3,185,881.25

The net profit for the first ten months this fiscal year, $1,268,
209.17.

In all probability the net profits of this year will exceed one
half of the total gross revenue of last year. Assuming the total
profit to be for this year $1,500,000, it would mean on the total
value of all wharves, sheds, approaches, roadways, office build-

ings, all equipment, the cotton warehouse, elevator, and coal tipple (not yet working) a net profit of 6½% after paying the interest on all outstanding bonds, with other words, the capital invested, and providing for maintenance, insurance funds and depreciation.

The Dock Board, limited in scope and vision and by law to give out only such bonds as for which earnings are in sight, can only by the the wildest stretch of terms and by further forcing the "Dock Board business" in the wildcat "profiteering gang" at great risk to the port business (33% of the revenue of the Dock Board is "profit") find foundation for a further issue of 15 million dollars of bonds, while the business of the port is right now starving for improvements amounting to an investment of 150 million dollars.

Those that shy at the magnitude of this sum may find comfort in some facts like the following:

New York is preparing to spend $1,000,000,000 in harbor improvements and commenced this spring with the Jamaica. Mill Bay harbor estimated to cost $150,000,000. For the city of Newark about 15 million dollars is being spent so that 260 acres may become a harbor.

Hamburg spent $10,000,000 for the Hamburg-American line alone, with splendid results. $34,000,000 were spent to secure for Rotterdam a better channel to the sea than the Rhine could give.

Amsterdam handling half New Orleans' tonnage only became a seaport at the cost of $38,000,000.

The inland port Duisburg built a coal harbor alone at the cost of $12,500,000.

Frankfort, 340 miles from the sea, with half New Orleans' population, spent $18,000,000 on her harbor.

Let us not look at the size of our task, but ask ourselves only: "Must it be done?"

SANITATION

Outside the harbor facilities there are other factors that affect a port. Such are the sanitary conditions of the city behind it. In the past New Orleans as a harbor was particularly handicapped by her unsanitary conditions, and if we don't look out, we will, without any consideration for splendid performance in

the past, drift back to a similar state. As late as July, 1914, we had the plague, and infected rats are still being caught here. We have rat-proofing ordinances which are, however, but spasmodically enforced. The city administration itself in violating them sets a poor example.

We collect our garbage in open cars, but do it as much on the sly as possible, scattering liberally their contents as they go on their way towards the dumps. We burn most of our garbage, weather permitting, the balance we conscientiously pile up as sanitation sentinels, around and in various parts of our city, and we are talking a great deal about improving upon it, and promise improvements some time next year, indicating that we are not entirely satisfied, which may be pardoned as we have right now a high typhoid mortality.

The surest way of eliminating our garbage dumps would be by locating one at the corner of St. Charles Avenue and State Street. We destroyed the breeding places of the yellow fever mosquito, and only a few clandestine cisterns exist in our midst, but give the mosquito a chance again in the tin cans of these garbage dumps. Some time we may eliminate other mosquito breeding places. We built a sewerage and water system which would stand favorably in comparison with other such systems in America, while the many miles of open drainage canals, like our garbage dumps, are carefully held far from our richest residential centers.

I have described our harbor facilities looked at, not with an all-condoning eye of a doting booster, but with the critical view of one who desires to show his love and trust in the future of New Orleans. I have set out to judge, not to find fault, offering as I went along suggestions which I believe give me the right to call my criticism constructive.

We must find economy, otherwise we must lose our foreign trade, and with that suffer greatly. Our present troubles are spelled, "Decline in Foreign Trade."

I gave the remedies as I went along, but they are all blocked until the Dock Board has "found" sufficient money out of their harbor charges, the Public Belt out of their charges to pay for these improvements.

The true remedy is our Industrial Canal and Inner Harbor.

NEW ORLEANS' INDUSTRIAL CANAL AND INNER HARBOR
ITS REASONS AND ADVANTAGES

While the first three chapters gave reasons why we may in a future not far distant, see 150 million tons of freight move through New Orleans, the fourth chapter laid bare how unprepared we are for any substantial increase of our harbor commerce, and how even the present day movement meets with difficulties and expenses due to insufficiency and inefficiency of our present freight handling facilities.

At the end of each of the preceding chapters I felt justified in pointing to New Orleans' Industrial Canal and Inner Harbor; it was this Inner Harbor that could prepare New Orleans for the new commerce; it was this Industrial Canal that could give us economy and efficiency.

This chapter is meant to show how this Industrial Canal can not only rectify all the errors of the past and substitute economy and efficiency for duplication and waste, but also how it may take care of this large future volume of freight.

In business life, economic law and necessity are the most irresistible of all forces, and to disregard the flow of economic currents or to go contrary to them is to court inevitable disaster.

The duplication of effort, inefficient use of space or equipment, leads only to greater confusion and expense. It is only by coordinating all agencies of transportation in their proper and scientific relation to each other and each in its most efficient way as part of a well-designed whole that economy can be realized, and opportunity for normal growth and expansion in the future be provided.

At present the harbor front, controlled by the unsatisfactory Dock Board excludes, unique to the entire world, all private ownership, private leases, and any development that might come under the protection of private interests. This had its advantages, but the disadvantages are now very serious, and can only be offset by delegating some field or region to private development, as is possible with the banks of, and land tributary to, the Industrial Canal.

Port facilities are no longer desired simply for the trans-shipment of foreign freight passing through a port, but in the service of a manufacturing and industrial terminal as well, g i v i n g a direct and permanent gain to the city owning the port.

It is generally recognized that the surest way to secure for a community permanent and r a p i d growth and prosperity is to encourage its industrial enterprises.

A harbor that is solely dependent upon commercial freight will have moments of great activities with sudden drops and idleness. The combination of industrial and commercial harbor, however, makes the freight movement in and out of the port far steadier; besides, in a general way, where 100 tons of commercial freight are needed per year to keep one family, producing ten tons of industrial freight will keep the same family. It has been the ideal of almost every port to create such combination, with very poor success on the part of all of them except New York.

The small percentage of manufactured products moving out of New Orleans is a great handicap to the steamship lines. The reason is that the agricultural, forest, mining and mineral products are bulky and ships leaving New Orleans often have a capacity cargo as far as the carrying capacity of the ship is concerned, but still have vacant space left in the hold.

Now with a fair balanced cargo, that is, with a fair percentage of manufactured products, it is possible to load a ship so that it will be loaded to its capacity and its cubic space filled, and since manufactured products always pay a higher freight rate than these low class commodities, one can readily see that the result of such loading means higher revenue for the steamer, which again means more advantageous ocean rates for the port, resulting in greater movement through the port.

One good way to attract industry has been to offer advantages of location in regard to transportation. In the United States the number of railroads entering the city has been the drawing card. In Europe the municipalities and the states have long since considered the rail transportation, under Government ownership or control, as a matter of course and have applied themselves to the development of water transportation as an additional attraction. The municipalities have gone to great expense to build and equip water transportation facilities in connection with industrial building sites.

They have sought to promote the common welfare by building the necessary harbor works and attracting to them the industries that are most interested in low freights. For instance, when the International Harvester Company was about to build a large factory

in Germany, Magdeburg offered an extensive area on the Elbe with a municipal wharf improvement included, in the very center of a great railroad net.

Neuss had tapped the Rhine water highway and built canal side arms and basins giving direct water-front to many acres of industrial sites.

The accessibility of raw materials was better at Neuss; at Magdeburg the distribution of the finished products was better. From this analysis, other things being equal, the Neuss location was better. Raw materials have a far less specific value, that is, greater weight and low value are less able to bear the traffic expense.

With the Industrial Canal, New Orleans combines the two advantages for a vast majority of industries.

The Industrial Canal permits the allocation of industrial harbor front and docks suitable for development peculiar to each need, each firm building and equipping its own harbor facilities as it deems necessary.

Keeping these principles in mind, let us consider the case of the industrial labor. The location of industry within the corporate limits of a municipality or a state is of great indirect advantage to that political unit. The industry pays wages and salaries to many persons who buy or rent homes and increase land values, which also increases the land tax income. The salaries and wages are spent in the shops and markets of the community, which increases the volume of business done, which again increases the income of the municipality, through the income and land taxes. The bank clearings are increased in the same manner, and with the same effects of quickening business and increasing the income of the local government by various direct and indirect methods of taxation.

Economy in ports, as cheapness in transportation, is a national asset because it helps to secure foreign trade. Foreign trade and increase in same is of the uppermost importance to us. We must expand or be forced to retreat from our present position with heavy losses all along the line—in shipping, banking and trade we are already ingloriously challenged by competitors in foreign markets. A courageous policy of legitimately aggressive development of all coordinated resources for the conduct of foreign trade is essential. There is no American who has not some stake in this struggle, be he capitalist, industrial, farmer or laborer.

World's permanent increase of wealth does not consist in foods, cotton, woolens, silks, clothing, beyond their per capita surplus; but in the winning of useful metals (such as iron, platinum, radium), docks, buildings, ships and such, and roads, tunnels, subways and canals that cheapen the cost of transportation.

It is for the same reason that the emptiness of our rivers is costly. Greater economy in our transportation is our laborers' greatest chance of not seeing their wages by force of necessity reduced to a too-low-standard.

The country that has the cheapest transportation is the most prosperous. One of the greatest necessities of economy in transportation is the coordination of all units of transportation. Build all the railroads, river lines, trunk lines, highways, and the merchant marine into one great system, one huge piece of machinery.

The marine road is the base road for all transportation. If the country is to go forward, if it is to maintain its present position, the means of transportation must be coordinated, not merely fitted one to another where they meet, but they must be so planned and ordered that they will constitute a single system directed to serve the country as a whole; and the same is true of a port.

With the Industrial Canal and Inner Harbor and the improvements at our river front suggested in Chapter 4, we may establish true economy in our harbor.

Efficiency in port equalizes greater distances, easily compensating for hundreds, yes thousands of miles of ocean voyage. The North Atlantic ports are 40% or about 1,500 miles nearer to North European ports than New Orleans.

Not only has New York a shorter distance to travel to Europe than New Orleans but to the east coast of South America, Africa and British and Dutch East India as well.

But in the total freight rate from farm to European ports the rail rates, four to eight times larger than the ocean rates, and second to that, the terminal charges play the important role.

Terminal costs, like every other burden upon the goods moved, have an unhappy faculty of multiplying rapidly. An unnecessary expense, bad enough in its original outlay, becomes pyramided until it adds several times its own amount to the cost of the article in the last market. The broker must add his charges to the goods handled with inadequate facilities, to cover freight shrinkage, profits and other items. The high terminal expense, caused by

70

inefficiency and parasites, swell the total of our national waste at every step.

The average expense of hauling a ton of freight 120 miles in the United States is equal to the expense of hauling the same ton of freight at the terminal.

To illustrate the little role the ocean freight rates play; the following examples may serve. Southeast Missouri produces Barytes. Her mines have long been successfully operated. Today Barytes, mined in Europe, is being delivered in New York cheaper than the freight which must be paid to carry Missouri Barytes to that point. Our competitors abroad are using cheaper forms of transportation and we can only respond by increasing rail rates. And if our foreign commerce is to continue, it must be aided by a rate of transportation which our waterways alone can afford to give.

New Orleans through high port efficiency and economies, and real efficient river transportation giving the low interior rates possible for us, can wipe out the discrepancies in sea distances for many a thousand miles.

But this must be done through real river transportation, not the "potential use", which latter is nothing else but scaring rail rates down, hurting the railroads, while sacrificing our true birthright, the river's economy. Besides, one can never beat the rail rates down to the real level of water transportation.

Thus New Orleans should find her greatest power in home economy, beyond outside influences, to the benefit of all the nation.

Many of our crimes against economy are absorbed by the railroads and it is generally felt that the absorption of the railroads rectifies such errors. Of course nothing is further from the truth. Even if such absorption were not finally visited in the rate structure of the port, even so it would be a crime against national economy returning with a vengeance in foreign harbors when competing with foreign manufacturers. But in many of the main trunk lines serving New Orleans no opportunity presents itself to recuperate from such expense except directly in the rates against the port and thus penalizing again the freight movement through our port. Again and again the sole answer is now and forever, home port economy. The best way of eliminating such waste is by eliminating through economy.

71

In industrial terminals every facility should be afforded for the rapid movement of freight between the factories and their storehouses and the wharves.

A map showing the present industries of New Orleans shows a surprising scattering, with the consequent expense of costly hauling and draying, causing a great many unnecessary switch tracks in New Orleans, with railroad crossings resulting in delays and interference in traffic.

The cart or dray is a necessary evil. Nothing should be moved by dray which can be moved by rail or lighter. The appreciation of this fact should cause port development to locate terminals, industries and warehouses so that drayage is reduced to a minimum.

As the factories need at various stages raw material, by establishing commodity harbors with warehouses, much of this drayage will be avoided.

The harbor facilities of New Orleans, like those of New York and all other American ports, suffer from extravaganza of space. Such lavish use of land, necessitating larger dray, switching and lighterage charges, is very detrimental to economy.

The Industrial Canal will save at least one, and in many instances a double and in some few cases a triple handling and drayage charge.

The Mississippi River does not afford full protection against weather, especially wind, which added to the great current, always constitutes a very decided danger, and so we may see sometimes two, three or even four times in one year, ships break away from control, causing in a few minutes tremendous damage, to become often a total loss when one of these vessels sinks in this ruthless stream.

The recent incident of the Tampa is a fair example of how one ship, maddened by the river current, when once broken loose, may play havoc with the other ships as a runaway horse in a china shop.

With an inner harbor this is eliminated, and this must eventually have a marked effect upon insurance rates.

Another advantage of the Industrial Canal is the practical elimination of pilferage, due to the possibility of enclosing the Canal and all its building by means of a factory fence. This pilferage is no small amount and runs to not less than $250,000 a year,

72

which entails an expense of not less than $350,000 a year to keep it at this level. This would warrant an investment of $7,000,000, could such investment completely eradicate this evil. The size of this leak need not astonish the reader if he only will consider our unprotected harbor front and absence of any river control or police boats. Only recently did I see beds under the wharves for the repose of the "wharf rats".

The Industrial Canal gives emancipation and freedom from public interference and the Dock Board; but permits private development and gives private initiative full sway.

A public harbor, publicly owned, without free play of private interest can never give the best dispatch, yet dispatch is of the uppermost value to a port.

Of two competitive ports having otherwise the same advantages, the port with the greatest dispatch is more readily used. And it stands to reason; steamships have cut their rates down so low that the margin of profit to the steamship owner is extremely small. Now suppose a vessel instead of lying three, seven or ten days here, is kept only one, four or five days, such saving may easily double the net revenue to the steamship owner and this would mean again lower rates to and from this port.

The Industrial Canal promotes such dispatch because it can give private enterprise free play. A public harbor never caters to any private need to such an extent as what would give the best dispatch. In the first place, new docks are not built in anticipation of new freight, but as the pressure of business forces. The actual wharf space is always behind the needs; the result is that it is often impossible, as has happened in New Orleans in the past, to definitely allocate a wharf until the vessel is in the river; so that the agent cannot in this manner accumulate the cargo and the loading of the ships or the unloading becomes directly dependable not only upon the speed and dispatch of the wharf, but of the railroad serving this wharf, causing delays and irregularities and consequently greater costs of loading.

Private ownership, or at least the assigning of space for long periods, to various companies, which the Industrial Canal can give, means that such companies could install the practical devices especially adaptable to their needs, so that they could give greater dispatch.

73

The Industrial Canal providing a constant level will make it possible to install such loading and unloading devices as are otherwise not economical, and loading and unloading cost will be greatly reduced from the cost now caused by the greatly varying water level at the river.

It is not enough that the port facilities keep abreast of immediate demands, the shipping capacity, as well as the quality of equipment of a port, must be well in advance of apparent requirements to handle its own commerce and to insure the maintenance of and improvements in its relative position with regard to other ports.

The Industrial Canal gives such elasticity of expansion.

Without the Industrial Canal, not only is the growth of New Orleans going to be scattered and confused, but the development of Valley trade will be scattered over many Gulf ports, certainly not to the nation's advantage, and to the detriment of economical handling and the development of New Orleans.

With the Industrial Canal the growth of New Orleans can be guided giving a great assistance in developing New Orleans along the ideal lines.

The Industrial Canal is the only sound solution for an economical terminal for river craft; it is only on the banks of a fixed level water channel such as this canal that true economy can be had for loading and unloading.

The Industrial Canal permits considerable investment in proper wharf equipment and the opportunity of concentrating such equipment at one point as needed.

The Industrial Canal is easily accessible to and from the city proper and gives an admirable passenger water route from the foot of Canal Street to Bayou St. John, New Basin and Mandeville.

The Industrial Canal gives a splendid opportunity for the development of an efficient lighterage system.

All of these needs can be fulfilled through the Industrial Canal and Inner Harbor and its reasons and advantages can be summed up as follows:

    (I)   As a drawing card to **industries,** offering:

        (a) ideal transportation conditions

        (b) economy in handling and shipment

        (c) ready supply of raw materials and fuel

        (d) easily accessible foreign markets.

(II) As an aid to our **freight carriers** through:
  (a) freedom to individual enterprise and from public board interference.
  (b) greater dispatch through more suitable facilities
  (c) greater safety against weather, thefts, and fire
  (d) cheaper loading cost through constant water level
  (e) greater elasticity for development
  (f) cheaper operation through coordinating, regulating and harmonizing of all handling, eliminating waste.

(III) As aid to the much needed **inland navigation** giving it:
  (a) proper terminal facilities
  (b) ready interchange of all traffic
  (c) a safe harbor for its equipment.

(IV) To foster **economy** and **efficiency** in our port:
  (a) through a lighterage system
  (b) reduction of drayage
  (c) elastic facilities
  (d) coordination of terminal carriers.

(V) For the city of **New Orleans** because it causes:
  (a) increase in our domestic and foreign trade
  (b) scientific, coordinated city development in lieu of haphazard growth
  (c) greater prosperity and activity
  (d) reduction of taxes
  (e) reduction of ocean rates
  (f) preparation for a larger volume of business.

(VI) For the **nation** because it gives it:
  (a) economy in one of its most important ports
  (b) increase in foreign trade by widening through economy and science the channel through which it must flow.

These then are the reasons and advantages of the Industrial Canal and Inner Harbor. The need of this canal has long been felt as can clearly be seen in the development of such places like Westwego, Amesville, Gretna, Harvey and Company Canal. It is no exaggeration to say that the prosperity of New York state is not only based upon but largely influenced by and due to the Erie Canal.

An industrial canal is not a new idea and has been advocated for New Orleans long long ago, although the idea has been buried and forgotten before the Civil War, to be revived again with the coming of the twentieth century. London, Antwerp, Danzig, offer illustrious examples. Danzig has created der Holm with a 30-foot deep cut-off of one of the loops of the Weichsel. Antwerp can point to the "Grand Coupoure" across the Scheldt where a lock canal is under construction, giving space for nine basins from 300 to 3,500 feet in length and 400 feet wide. Frankfort on the Main spent $18,000,000 for a 110-acre inner harbor.

What such a canal may do to the future of a city is best illustrated by such examples as Rotterdam and Manchester, the latter of which spent $80,000,000 to bring the ocean vessels to its doors.

Unlike Philadelphia, Boston and New York, New Orleans has not fought in any way transportation improvements that would benefit other communities.

Competition between harbors is largely a territorial proposition calling for close cooperation on the part of related interests.

New Orleans by heeding this great truth can and must come into its own without stooping to the nefarious practice of other communities.

Let the river front be the nursery for the Inner Harbor. The Industrial Canal to be New Orleans' stomach. Under this plan, all necessary warehouses and docking facilities on our river front, publicly owned can be operated on a basis of actual cost of service, giving each shipper and carrier absolutely the same treatment, eliminating duplication's wastefulness and the railroad competition at terminals, which has given such highly unsatisfactory results, and full sway given to private development on the Industrial Canal and Inner Harbor.

HISTORY AND DESCRIPTION OF THE INDUSTRIAL CANAL

It is difficult to speak about the Industrial Canal without going into some of its history and the power that made it materialize.

While the need of a direct water connection between Lake Pontchartrain and the Mississippi River was felt in the past by a chosen few, notably by Bienville and Carondelet, it had remained dormant from pre-Civil War days, to be brought to the fore again in 1902 with new vigor and strengthened with modern reasons by a young man who believed in New Orleans, but saw its problems and difficulties, and in his quiet but effective and determined way set out to bring these problems to a solution.

A profound student of economics, provided with an unusually broad, constructive mind, he tackled one by one the "hooks on New Orleans" that prevented "coordination of forces of economy". Step by step he fought New Orleans' battles, sometimes alone, sometimes as general, sometimes as private in the ranks, but always following a careful, prearranged plan, and marking New Orleans' highway to success with victories as milestones, such as the victory for a sane quarantine law, a final and decisive one against yellow fever, eradication of the plague, use of our waterways, development of foreign trade, while the fight for a model water, sewer and drainage system saw him in the front ranks. Sometimes wrong in detail, always right in principle, this man has done more for the business of this great community than all its business men combined. His name shall forever indelibly be written squarely across the pages of the history of New Orleans' Industrial Canal and Inner Harbor, and to many ears its waters shall murmur his name in praise. This man, to whom a member of a former Dock Board once attributed a "telescopic view", saw clearly that this Industrial Canal alone could remove many of the difficulties facing the commerce of New Orleans.

While the linking of Lake Pontchartrain with the river at New Orleans was ever in the minds of leaders of this community, the greater functions of such a canal as the Industrial Canal and Inner Harbor were not always considered, and often not even realized in the idea of connecting these two bodies of water, creating a canal as a link in the great inter-coastal canal scheme alone.

It was under this delusion that the Lake Borgne Canal was commenced shortly after the Civil War, but because it merely con-

nected the Mississippi River through Lake Borgne with the Mississippi Sound, and because its fourteen miles distance from New Orleans severely handicapped the idea of an Inner Harbor and Industrial area, it was never a success.

Where the purpose of the earlier plans was simply to build a connecting waterway, the object of this great canal, now nearing completion, is to create industrial development.

The main motive behind the Industrial Canal was a solution of the difficulty which arose from the Spanish and French treaties under which none of the river front can be sold or leased to private enterprise. It was publicly admited by business leaders and press alike that the lack of that canal has proven to have cost the city already much in trade and industry.

On February 10, 1918, a committee consisting of thirteen of the most prominent men of New Orleans urged the immediate construction of the canal as provided for by the Constitutional amendment of November, 1914, on the ground that

(I) It will provide fixed level water front sites for commerce and industries,

(II) Permit private development,

(III) Permit coordination of river, rail and sea traffic,

(IV) It will develop lighterage, provide opportunity for a free port and foster the creation of markets of deposit,

(V) Give New Orleans a safe, fixed-level harbor,

(VI) Serve as link in the Intercoastal Canal.

In this we find the echo of the oft-repeated statements of the man who for over twenty years saw the great need of this Industrial Canal and who deliberately made his life task to hasten, to the extent within his power, the coming of New Orleans into her rightful place—the leading port of the world, both in size and economy.

Originally the canal was not planned by the Dock Board to be as large as it is now reaching completion. The first plans provided for a barge canal, the cost of the lock was figured at $1,400,000, and that of digging the canal $1,250,000. The land was bought for $1,500,000, at an average rate of $1,665 per acre.

However, gradually the dimensions of lock and canal were increased, due to the insistence of the engineering firm responsible, until it now provides for a navigable draft of 27 feet with a possible increase to 30 feet as soon as the canal is dredged to 35 feet, the

78

lock giving a water depth over its miter sill of 30 feet already. In total, the cost of the canal will more readily pass the $25,000,000 mark than remain under this.

Coming from the river a ship is first confronted with a steel bascule bridge, four of which now cross the Industrial Canal. The one at the lock is very inadvisedly placed, only 150 feet away from the outer gate, and will interfere greatly with the lockages and in return be considerably interfered with by same. For every large ship going through the lock, this bridge will be open not less than ten, possible twenty minutes. Such large ship passing through the lock will not proceed under her own power, but is pulled by means of six capstans, capable of developing a pull just about strong enough to move the larger vessels at very slow speed. But this also means shifting and placing cables, all time-costing operations. No captain or pilot would dare to bring his ship to the lock unless the bridge stood open awaiting him. So either he will have to moor before the bridge and await his turn, or the open bridge must be awaiting him as he enters the canal, and even then prudence, nay, absolute necessity will demand that the ships slide in and are pulled into the lock at no greater speed than one mile an hour. That speed he should have from a point certainly not less than a thousand feet away from the lock gates.

Thus I believe that should nothing go wrong and everything move serenely, the bridge must remain open for each lockage from ten to fifteen minutes, perhaps even twenty minutes. Now, during high water with perhaps only four feet clearance, necessitating bridge opening for every craft and launch, the chances are that even in the first year of the canal an average of two lockages per hour may be needed as has been often the case with the little Lake Borgne Canal. And if traffic develops anywhere near the tonnage I feel safe in predicting, or if traffic develops anywhere near the amount that would have justified the construction of the canal, the bridge will occasionally be available for street traffic.

The lock is wonderfully built out of very solid concrete; but the ship has received little consideration. The kinetic energy of a ship of 2,500 tons, moving at a speed of one mile per hour, or one and one-half feet per second, is little appreciated by the layman, but little excuse is lett for the engineering firm responsible for the design who lets this ship strike solid concrete with an impact of 350 foot-tons, not damaging the concrete, but very much the one-

half inch plates of the ship that may receive the blow between the frames. While the blow would be ten times larger for the ship of the lock's capacity, chances are that she would only receive a glancnig blow on account of the snugger fit. An elastic pile structure outside bridge and locks may greatly assist here but nevertheless, I criticise severely the fact that the lock itself offers little else but solid stone to meet the ship. Much can yet be done to alleviate the consequences of this error, but this will be patch-work and nothing else.

A great deal of pride is based upon the fact that this lock has five gates and two emergency gates—an absolutely unnecessary wasteful multiplication.

If Holland can find itself safe in every one of its eight sea locks behind a single set of gates with the North Sea often lashed by western storms to fury breaking against them, I fail to see the need of this multiplication of gates and emergency dams.

The Amsterdam North Sea Canal gates built in sand have 40 feet of water over the sill and 80 feet usable width, 40% larger surface than the Industrial Canal gates. The land behind them is 10 feet below sea level, and in a furious wertern storm the sea aganist the gates often towers 30 feet above the densely populated rich land behind it.

If an emergency dam is absolutely wanted, why not build an effective one? Any one knows that it is the mad onward rush of water that does the damage, not the dead water a f t e r it is confined. And unless emergency gates are automatic and become immediately effective as soon as needed, they are of only little, or even doubtful value. Moreover, the working of the present emergency dam sounds nice in theory, but he that can picture the protecting beams sliding peacefully and correctly into place while a w'ld, raving torrent tears its way through the lock, has more imagination than engineering knowledge. For an effective operation it must be necessary that the man who is to operate the crane to place the dam is for day after day, month after month, year after year on the job and alert — he must not lose his head when suddenly, like thunder, the fatal moment comes; he must not stumble when running to the crane from table or toilet, his nerve must hold and neither should he blunder. Much safety against this may be found in three double-watch shifts at the cost of $6,000 a year in wages, and when this human

element does not fail, but responds after so many hundred thousand hours of waiting and electric power does not fail at the closing of the switch, then it should prove possible for these nine beams to evenly slide into place, not held or disarranged by current, whirlpool, sand, bending, debris, logs, boats and everything else sucked in this wild raving vortex. Did I say such man had imagination? A mistake — he lacks every vestige of it. He could not picture to himself the power of the giant. The only possible effective emergency gate is the sleeping one, embedded in the lock floor, forced up by heavy current, held in check and retarded by uncoiling springs, chains and buffers, but ever ready day or night, never waiting for sleeping, absent, wounded or panic-striken operators or failing power, but watchful like its enemy, the river itself, waiting for its opportunity.

If the emergency dam were only meant to be used in case of needed repairs, another phase offers itself. The present gates are so constructed that their interior is accessible. Generations should pass, if the locks are well constructed, before any other repairs should be required as may be learned from the Kiel, North Sea, Soo, Welland, Manchester Canal, etc. Why then spend now $380,000 which, under the existing circumstances, will have doubled in eleven years, and in twenty-two years quadrupled itself on equipment that deteriorates when in such case it would have sufficed to build the two slots in the wall, so that whenever such repair really proves necessary the dam beams can be constructed and then paid for and placed in the slot by hired land or floating-cranes? That is, providing one should insist upon such type of emergency gate as is now installed. Another type than that one or the first one that I suggested could have been hinged beams hoisted from a recess into place like a curtain runing over rollers, the hoisting automatically starting when the current exceeds a certain velocity.

With our public monopoly of harbor frontage, there are no investments to restrain any steamship line from pulling stakes and moving to other ports. 127 miles of heavy river current from sea to the foot of Canal Street is no small handicap; sufficient at any rate to bring Galveston considerably nearer to the Florida and Yucatan channel than New Orleans geographically is.

Little does the average man realize by what costly and precarious channels our harbor is connected with the sea. Never sure of ·

81

the required depth especially during high river stage it would not take a great or peculiar accident to rob New Orleans' harbor of a connection with the sea.

The "Detroit" wreck came very near closing us completely in when the "Arizona" veered over her.

Generations of constant labor and vigilance and 18 million dollars have not brought us much further from this danger point.

It is now believed by the Army Engineers in charge of this difficult and problematic work that a year from now Southwest Pass may give 30 instead of 20 feet of water, then supporting South Pass, but, granting that this comes to be true, the passes shall never cease to worry all men in charge and depending upon them.

If ever the passes fail New Orleans for only a short period its commerce must suffer a staggering blow.

Towage, bar and river pilotage, 127 miles of river current and crooked channel place a burden upon New Orleans shipping easily equal to 10^c a ton carrying capacity, or about three times the difference between American and foreign seamen's wages, which differential is so often given as cause of our decline of ocean shipping.

If now the Industrial Canal and Inner Harbor is used, there must be added to this handicap the time loss of lockage and passage through the canal, three bridges and syphon spurs.

All of this points to a sea channel from the lake end of the canal to the Gulf. I believe this channel should follow the lake shore to' Point Aux Herbes lighthouse, from there to West Rigolets lighthouse, through the Rigolets, passing Long Point lighthouse and Pearl River lighthouse, through Grand Island Pass, south of Cat Island to north of Chandeleur Island, joining southwest of Ship Island with the Gulfport channel, a total distance of 75 miles, as against a river route of 127 miles. A channel 40 feet deep, 1,000 feet in width, with levees to the Rigolets, and 2,000 feet width with slow sloping banks should not cost more than $18,000,000, less by half what it cost the Government to create an 8–foot channel between Rock Island and Moline, Illinois, a distance of ten miles.

The outer levee a hundred and fifty feet wide, protected by piling and concrete mattresses would serve as a splendid roadway between New Orleans and the state of Mississippi.

82

The government has had for years on its program the construction of an intercoastal canal.

Let the state of Louisiana declare the Industrial Canal a free canal and let the Government spend the funds intended for this intercoastal canal as part of this protected deep sea channel. Vessels may then enter the Industrial Canal from the sea through the lake, avoiding locking and the St. Claude bridge.

The cross section of the canal is a trapezoid, the parallel sides being the water level and bottom. Between river and lock the bottom is 150 feet and the water level 275 feet wide, between the lock and the lake the water level will be 300 feet with a 150 feet wide bottom.

Up till now it has been planned to give the canal a depth of 30 feet in the erroneous belief that such depth corresponds with the depth of 30 feet over the miter sill of the lock. This is of course not so, as it is an entirely different matter for a ship to slide in or out of a concrete tub even with her bottom only barely missing the sill, than to try to navigate a fairway with such little leeway. Squatting, attraction, loss of steering power through water displacement would make such navigation impossible. A depth of 30 feet over the miter sill calls at least for a depth of 35 feet in the canal.

A canal of trapezoid cross section is one solely used for navigation channels since it does not permit vessels to approach the banks. Vessels of the same depth as this canal must remain 75 feet from from either shore. For this reason alone must the canal cross section be a rectangle which necessity is emphasized by the needs of navigation. A vessel of 30 feet draft has a beam ranging from 50 to 60 feet and sometimes more; two such vessels would have no space left between themselves for practical navigation, if the canal bottom keeps either 75 feet from shore. But even for one vessel alone, the needs of navigation are such that the rectangular cross section must be adopted. A ship negotiating the canal must be able to maintain a speed sufficient for steering purposes and the channel must be wide enough to permit such speed.

If further due allowance is made for ample manoeuvering space for all other craft that will ply upon the canal when fully in use, and thought is given to the fact that at such later date it will prove imposs'ble, at least impractical, to set the structures in the meantime created on the canal banks back so as to widen the canal,

it seems imperative that now the proper width be provided. This should be not less than 500 feet. To navigate such channel 500 feet wide at water level and bottom, 35 feet deep with large ocean vessels drawing 30 feet, while many smaller craft are plying about, will still demand a great deal of skill and ability, unprotected as the canal is against all winds; yet navigation cannot very well be stopped because a breeze is blowing.

The intended cross section of the canal has not yet been reached, the dredging being done to about 55%. To change the proposed channel to an usable one corresponding with the dimensions of the lock, that is a rectangular channel 500 feet wide and 35 feet deep, would mean a cross section 2.6 times larger than the present accepted one. The work so far done would be 21% of that necessary channel. In other words, about one-fifth of the channel required is dredged so far. To make such a channel, fourteen and a half million cubic yards more dredging must be done than has already been accomplished, at a cost of 5^c per yard, or $725,000.

The rectangular cross section essential for this canal requires a bank revetment which I estimate to cost about $3,000,000. The revetment construction should keep time with the channel dredging.

The dredging could be done in four months by four large 20-inch suction dredges, providing the first dredging removed all cypress stumps and providing further it remains possible to dump all dredged material on the east bank of the canal, with the advantage of thus simultaneously raising this land.

The canal should further be provided with a double roadway, at the canal property line costing about $625,000, a complete telephone system, a series of mooring posts near bridges, canal entrances and locks, mooring bolders in the canal, and a lighting system, bringing the total additional cost of the canal including dredging, revetment, contingencies and other minor needs not yet provided for to $6,000,000.

With the improvements suggested the canal can be brought into splendid condition while the St. Claude bridge may be avoided through the use of a deep sea approach through Lake Pontchartrain and Rigolets.

METHODS AND POLICIES RELATING TO
THE USE OF THE CANAL

The uses of the Industrial Canal and Inner Harbor can be classified as its name implies under two main headings; (a) Inner Harbor, (b) as Industrial Basin.

As Inner Harbor it must shelter the steamship lines, the deposit markets of Valley and foreign products through a large number of warehouses, and give an unexampled opportunity for a free harbor with corresponding drawing power for industries foreign to our shores.

Many of the steamship lines having no investment here, have substantial properties, wharves, docks, cranes, etc., in other ports they serve. They made such investments because they found it advantageous and paying to their business. Given a free hand and encouragement they will gladly avail themselves of the opportunity to do here likewise.

They should be permitted to build such facilities as they feel particularly the need of. They cannot do so on a twenty-year lease. This would mean an uncertainty of location and the necessity of burdening their annual expense with a sinking fund of 3% of the investment made on such leased property. Besides the greater economy possible to them on this canal, they must be assured permanency and freedom from interference of any outside source.

The contract with one of the two enterprises that ventured so far upon the Industrial Canal had a clause that gave the Dock Board the right to fix any day during the first six months of each year, rental for that year, the lessee when not satisfied with such decision had four months time to remove its belongings, finished and unfinished work included. Although the Dock Board admits that it received inquiries from over a hundred large enterprises, it has not yet completed and announced any policy covering the manner in which the canal may be used, and only a few months ago opined in writing that investigations leading to such policy were premature. However it did bind itself in a report published by it in May of this year to a policy that the frontage on the canal must be developed before there is any extensive construction of lateral basins and slips. This will tend to confusion and serious problem in the future

85

The canal used as Inner Harbor means that the various steamship lines may develop private docks, sheds and wharves, equipped to suit their needs with such mechanical devices as they desire.

These harbor sites will be served by lighters, public belt, barge lines and street. The saving per ton through elimination or reduction of charges for sheddage, wharfage, dockage, demurrage, switching, draying, pilferage, insurance and stevedoring and the important saving of ships' time, as is possible through private endeavor, should range from $2 to $3.50 per ton.

The steamship company may for instance construct itself a U-form, open to the canal, wharf. The inner length to be equal to not less than the greatest length of ship it desires to accomodate. The width of the slip between the two legs of the U to be not less than twice the width of the widest vessel that will use it plus 120 feet. The width of each leg to be about 130 feet, making the length of land side of the U 500 feet more or less.

Use alternately one leg for inbound cargo, the other leg for outbound. Make the wharf or pier building two or more stories. Supply Burton tackles, cranes, cargo masts, conveyors, telphers etc., etc., as may be needed; provide a single rail track in the center of each leg, the one in the right leg of the building leaving it to the right, the other to the left. The longitudinal halves of two stories of each leg of the U provide enough cargo space for a 12,000 ton vessel with goods tiered 15 feet, not figuring on the removal of any goods by trains, lighters, barges or drays. The drays can deliver and receive goods unmolested by trains in the main building. Barges to receive and deliver at the end of each of the legs and lighters to receive from or deliver to ships or wharf at will. With such building a despatch of two days for the largest size vessel that comes to New Orleans is possible.

Such building with all its track, slips and approaches would not occupy more than 10 acres in total. It would only require 700 feet of length of the Industrial Canal and would have a combined delivery and receiving capacity without working overtime of 3,000.000 tons per year. Suppose further that the Dock Board charged $10,000 per acre (if it can be made legally possible to sell the land; otherwise it should levy a rental and sinking fund based upon that valuation with a lease running over a larger period than the law now allows) it could place 24 such buildings

86

—

and have still room for sufficient laterals. These combined buildings should have a yearly capacity of 72 million tons. The Dock Board would receive for the frontage alone 24 x $100,000 = $2,400,000. This should be all the charges against the steamship lines which must themselves pay for the wharf construction and its equipment, making a total cost of about $2,900,000, and together with the land value (which indeed represents a small percentage of the total cost), a sum of $3,000,000. Maintenance, insurance, depreciation and interest total at 10% per year means that the steamship lines would have to meet for such ideal condition an annual charge of $300,000 or 10^c per ton of the wharf's capacity, considerably less then what they now pay in general dock board charges.

With this equipment it should be able to give a fourfold quicker dispatch to its vessels certainly equal to not less than 15 to 20^c per ton, avoid expensive hauling about, save considerable on Public Belt and warehouse charges, reduce pilferage and insurance and last but not least, cut the handling cost such as loading, unloading, stevedoring, hauling and watching not less than $1 per ton in the average.

It is well, however, not to base the finances of the canal on this Inner Harbor development, as this is going to be a slow process.

The next development must come on land connected with the Canal set aside for warehouse and free zone basin. This branch of harbor activities should find its home as near the present business center of New Orleans as possible and must therefore be located on the west bank of the canal as near the locks as possible. Its location is very definitely predetermined by conditions, and is between Grant Street and North Claiborne Avenue. This work and development falls very clearly under the Dock Board's authority.

The Dock Board should provide here a warehouse basin where it places at the disposal of private warehousemen flour, rice, coffee, tobacco, sisal, fur, rubber, jute, cotton and many other commodity and cold storage warehouses to be held on long time general leases, built with the money advanced by the lessee and operated along general lines, rules, regulations laid down by the Dock Board.

With an abundance of warehouses the Industrial Canal will become a market of deposit, with the result that materials will

give preference to being carried in storage in this Industrial Canal Zone, the receipts for which certified to and insured by reliable concerns, may be traded in the world over. This means the bringing of capital to New Orleans, and again the inducement of industries to locate here, as they can then buy and deliver in a spot market, taking advantage of the most suitable quotations. These warehouses will give birth to a new business here—that of wharfingers, which is so highly and successfully developed in Europe.

The Dock Board may decide to build the warehouses out of its own funds, in which case it should fix the applying tariffs and contract for the operation of these warehouses with the highest bidder.

The free zone adjacent to this warehouse basin must of necessity remain under general Dock Board control. The Dock Board either leasing sites, furnishing plants, warehouses or lofts to manufacturers on short or long term leases. The Dock Board should figure in its charges for the site $10,000 per acre over and above the real estate cost and cost of construction of basin, warehouses or factories.

We may also create at the Industrial canal bonded warehouses, and factitious bonded warehouses not controlled by the customhouse authorities. The factitious bonded warehouse should hold goods liable to low duties, which goods the customhouse authorities confine themselves to, controlling the quantities stored there from time to time.

The land around the present turning basin where the shipyard of the Foundation Company is located must be turned over to all passenger services, be it for lake, river or ocean.

Provisions to be made for customhouse and immigration needs, and perfect connection with the city and the Union passenger depot by means of road, trolley and railroad cars. All vessels permitted and encouraged to load and discharge their passengers there at a charge sufficient for operation, maintenance and sinking funds.

All remaining land west of the canal and north of Florida Walk to be designated for food, fruit, fish harbors, canning and general manfacturing center, and for general power plant serving these industries, the free zone and warehouses.

While all of this land should be charged with one prime underlying charge of $10,000 per acre, it should be further charged for all developments created there by the Dock Board.

It is on this land west of the canal and on the canal bank where the second phase of New Orleans harbor management should find expression: the system of public ownership and private operation, in contrast with the first phase, on the river, where we have public operation and ownership and the third phase east of the canal where there must be established private ownership and private operation.

No serious study has yet been made by the present Dock Board of the manner in which it will charge for the use of the canal. Will it charge to meet the interest and operating charges or will it accept a yearly loss? if so, how much, and for how long? Will it charge tolls, lockage, rental per lineal foot, or per acre, charge per lateral, per freight ton or capacity ton?

What ever method of charges is decided upon it must be in accordance with following unqualified principles:

I. The ultimate returns from the canal should suffice to retire all the bonds the Dock Board ever issued on canal and river alike and refund the accumulated interest paid on the canal bonds.

II. A certain estimated period, must be fixed within which the estimated development must have paid for these bonds and interest.

III. The unit over which these costs must be divided must be such that it can under proper development increase to keep the charge per unit down.

IV. The charge should not exceed an agreed upon percentage of the economic margin of the Canal's advantages.

V. Charges should be so planned as causing a minimum of supervision, of administration, interference with the free flow of commerce, and collection cost, and should in preference be applied only once.

VI. Such principles cannot be carried out unless a definite plan of development for this harbor governing the period fixed in II is adopted.

The following facts have led to the adoption of these six basic principles. It seems logic that the industries deriving benefits from the Canal should pay in full for the canal, otherwise it would be in fact a grant of public funds to private enterprise. But in view of the benefits that must be derived by New Orleans and Louisiana from the new industries located here on account of the canal and therefore the desirability to place as few difficulties as possible in the way of these new industries, but quite

to the contrary to hold out as many inducements as possible to them, it seems proper to charge these industries cost and interest but no more.

The canal has so many advantages over the river front that care should be taken that provision is made against a sudden replacment of commerce from the river to the canal leaving the river Dock Board bonds without ample revenue. It seems equally important that the canal should share with the river front some of its economic advantages and for these reasons all ultimate users of the canal combined should bring forth into the Dock Board's treasury a sum equal to **all** Dock Board bonds (river as well as canal), with all interest paid accumulated and accrued upon the canal bonds.

How are we going to determine now who all the users are, in what manner are we going to get a line on them, and what is the sum they must ultimately pay? That is, what period of years must pass before all moneys have been returned so that we may fix the amount of interest, the principle being fixed?

We have a very definite check upon the Canal beneficiaries as we know where they must locate, neglecting the users who merely pass through the canal, they having paid their compensation through the proposed Government-made deep sea channel through the lake.

The bonds draw 5% interest and the cost of maintenance, administration and operation of the canal may be placed at about $375,000 equal to an additional 1½% per year.

The outstanding canal bonds by the time the canal is finished will amount to $25,000,000. Assuming that the repayment of this fund is gradually, over the period agreed upon under principal II at 17 years then the principal and interest and the $13,500,000 river bonds would combined amount to $51,000,000 the repayment to average $3,000,000 per year. The only satisfactory solution to meet principal III, IV and V is the use of the developed land tributary to the canal. This would mean that for 17 years a minimum average of 300 acres of land tributary to the canal must qualify for change into harbor land by paying into the Dock Board's treasury $10,000 per acre. There remains to be seen whether this is practical.

The above revenue must come from the industrial harbor function of the canal.

The west and center development, that of public utilities and steamship lines will be slow, and must be fostered and nursed by the Dock Board. The revenue can likewise come in slowly because it is this portion of the canal (the harbor part) which refunds the outstanding river bonds, but as the interest on these bonds is met by the river itself and the necessity of liquidating these river bonds keep pace with the development of this inner harbor, no undue haste need to be shown in forcing this inner harbor development. What is, however, needed is a definite plan covering this land.

It is the land east of the canal that must be developed as industrial center. It is here where private enterprise, ownership and operation must have full sway.

What opportunity can we offer industries here? which industries? and what value are these opportunities to these industries? What response may be expected to this? That is, in what numbers and in what lapse of time? These are now the vital questions. Correct answers to these questions are needed to decide upon the canal plans and finances.

The opportunity we can offer comes under three headings: Transportation, raw materials and markets.

In all three groups we can offer on the Industrial Canal the **ideal.**

It is at the Industrial Canal where ocean and the world's best river system meet in quiet fold. A magnificient fan-like radiating railroad system, its rates held down through easy construction, competes with inland navigation, giving the best of service to three-fourths of the United States, that basin lying between the Rocky and Appalachian Mountains, the Great Lakes and the Gulf, in which surges this ever increasing spring of manufactured, mineral, agricultural, and forests products; now containing the center of population of the United States seeking the center of the Valley. While the Atlantic Coast must artificially pump its commerce from this basin, the Industrial Canal, through the magnificent water and rail system can readily tap it.

Public belt, the concentrated railroad system, lighters, barge lines, drays and trucks may meet deep sea vessels of all ports of the world under truly ideal conditions of economy, safety and efficiency.

Terminal charges are always a very important part of the transportation cost, and are at an absolute minimum in the Industrial

91

Basin. Each industry, through complete ownership will be given the fullest opportunity to develop and install the best handling devices it decides upon.

While the meeting of exterior transportation lines in the Industrial Canal is most felicitous, the interior transportation system of the Industrial basin need not be any less so. The plan for the construction of this Industrial basin when finally adopted by the Dock Board must and will protect and secure this important point so that the utmost benefits are derived from the juxtaposition of the industries among themselves. Such judicial planning shall take full benefits of this virgin field and see to it that the raw materials for each plant are secured at a minimum of cost, and if possible as the by-products of another industry.

Louisiana soil produces many important raw materials especially for the chemical industry. Louisiana is the only territory where sulphur, salt, cotton, petroleum and gas are found at each other's side, the four prime basic chemicals for almost every chemical industry, such as dyes, explosives, sulphuric acids, glass, bleaches, soaps, drugs, celluloid, etc.

Not only are these raw materials, through water transportation, practically at the harbor's gates, but this very same cheap water transportation brings us the many other raw products from adjoining states such as bauxite, lime, koalin, fluorspar, coal, pig iron, cement, gold, tungsten ore, vanadium, zinc, silver, lead, manganese ore, marble, mica, phosphate, fuller's earth, pumice, barytes, quicksilver, copper, pyrite, etc., all of which articles can be more cheaply concentrated at the Industrial Canal than anywhere else, supplementing the raw materials of Louisiana already named and to which should be added the other Louisiana products such as lumber and other forest products, lignite, asphalt, silica and other mineral products.

Finally, New Orleans being the gateway, can cheaper than any other community collect the needed imported raw material, especially those from the Southern Hemisphere, such as: hides, furs and other animal propucts, fruits, nuts, coffee and other plantation products, tropical and western states lumber, rubber, foreign chemicals such as annato, balsams, chicle, divi-divi, logwood dyes, mangrove bark, medical plants, nitrates, petigrain, important minerals such as cuban ores, asbestos, bismuth, borates, chrome, cobalt, manganese, mercury, nickel, tin, gypsum and porphyry.

Louisiana's agricultural products give New Orleans the unique advantage of being able without importation to feed its industrial population.

To these easily accessible raw materials and foods, the markets of the world are closely brought at the Industrial Canal through the many ocean lines finding here balanced cargos, and abundance of freight. This then together with the unexcelled opportunity of developing an ideal harbor in virgin field especially and admirably suitable for harbor purpose, giving together with the river, the lake and canal the most ideal harbor sites, we offer to new industries. Particularly the following industries must heed the opportunity offered them: The steel, lumber, oil, coal, rubber, chemical, stockyards, clothing and cordage and we shall see rise to the east of the canal a steel, lumber, oil, coal, rubber, chemical, stockyard and clothing harbor. To the west of the canal in the food harbor we shall see the chocolate, macaroni, margarine industries thrive. The imported vegetable oils and the new chemical industry is going to give us the new soap industry of territory F named on page 33. There is no single reason why Cincinnati should have preference over the Industrial Canal for the fabrication of soap. We can import cheaper than it the necessary ingredients and add to this the by-products of our stockyard industry, brought to the Industrial Canal for export reasons. Cattle is brought cheaper and better by water to the Industrial Canal from the Western States than to Chicago.

Cuban ore is carried to Kill van Kull, New Jersey, thence via Lehigh Valley Railroad to Bethlehem, Penn., and meets Pennsylvania coal there. Again Cuban ore is carried to Sparrow's Point, Md., and meets Virginia coal there carried to it by rail.

For less money that these two rail charges coal can be carried by barges from Alabama, Kentucky, and Illinois to the Industrial Canal, while Cuban ore could be carried to the Industrial Canal for less than the cost of carrying it to either of the above named harbors. Limestone is found on the banks of the Warrior. Texas too yields desirable ores. With freedom from political interference how reasonable would be the location of a blast furnace adjacent to the Industrial Canal. The cost of fabricating the pig iron and ingots would be as cheap as in Birmingham with a decided advantage for export loaded right at the plant in ships coming along side its docks and loading cheaper than now is done else-

93

where in the United States. A plant so located could save from $2 to $3 per ton of finished products.

Undoubtedly this industry has been kept away from New Orleans because there was simply no place for it, the entire harbor being under political control and excluding any private enterprise. Even under adverse conditions New Orleans without such blast furnaces here exported last year close to 80,000 tons in pig iron and steel billets.

This was because New Orleans better than any other Gulf port could offer the general cargo that would best go with such heavy iron and steel products, adding thus another advantage of such plant here.

Such blast furnaces would surely bring with them coke by products plants, and steel and rolling mills.

Salt like sulphur is a basic chemical for almost every chemical industry. With our own raw materials so cheaply brought to the Industrial Canal we shall make caustic soda, chlorine, bleaches, soda ash, cooking soda, Glauber's salt. With the bauxite from White River, Arkansas, or Rome, Georgia, all carried by water if necessary, we shall make in our new Industrial Canal Zone metallic alumium, and alumium and tin-ware, with the aid of our steel industry. Carborundum, calcium carbide, calcium, cyanide, nitric acid, ammonia, chloroform, iodoform, hydrogen, oxygen, phosphorus, and carbon disulphide shall be made in our chemical harbor. The oil refineries, dyestuffs and explosives call for heavy chemicals made from salt and sulphur. If Germany can master in thirty years 95% of the world's chemical industry, importing sulphur from Sicily, salt from Austria, cotton from America and Egypt, and oil from Upper Silesia, we can do better here. Our 99.8% pure sulphur must give us sulphuric acid by the contact process, by which process concentrated acid is made direct without subsequent evaporation, other products are sulphur dioxide for our sugar industry, carbon disulphide, thiosulphates, etc.

The cotton fiber is the purest natural form of cellulose, giving us nitrocellulose or explosives, artificial silk, waterproof sheets, artificial leather, pegamoid, patent leather, collodion, celluloid, (films,) transparant curtains for automobiles, etc. lacquer for highly polished instruments, and a body for aluminum paint.

94

The cotton seed gives us cotton seed meal, cotton seed oil hogless lards, hard fats, soap making, glycerine, and with imported vegetable oils, margarine.

Our 52 billion feet of long-leaf yellow pine and our 15 billion feet of short-leaf yellow pine, our cypress and other hardwoods, are going to give us with the aid of other raw material imported and by-products: grain alcohol, paper, producer gas, artificial silk, nitrocellulose, cattle food, tannin extracts, rosin, turpentine, pine oils, spirits, rosin oils, pheneloids, crude wood alcohol, acetone, unbleached pulp.

Our gypsum will give us cement plasters, hard wall finishes, plate glass, land plaster. Lignite, sand, gravel, clays with its bricks and tiles, limestone which gives us bleaching powder should the electrolytic production of chlorine be located in sufficient nearness, all found in Louisana around our waterways help in emphasizing the fact the chemical industry must find here its Mecca.

Is there any reason why we should carry New Orleans' sand to Shreveport to make glass there instead of piping the natural gas to New Orleans?

Is there any reason why we should make poor matches in America or import good ones from Europe when at the Industrial Canal we can bring the phosphate rocks from Florida, the Louisiana sulphur and the lumber all by water?

Why should we continue to ship the raw rubber through New Orleans to Akron to meet there the cotton from the South, to return to us the finished tires for export, tying to this export trade such frightful and needless handicap?

The Sabine district developed in nine years to the most important oil harbor of America. New Orleans would have no difficulty in regaining this lost field. The oil industry would gladly concentrate here if we had an efficient oil harbor and pipe line to it. A harbor confined, free of current, would not only make an economical harbor but a safe one as well, eliminating the dangers of floating oil.

With our salt we should make our own chlorine and bleaches, bringing here the textile industries to our cotton market instead of shipping our raw cotton away. With our bleaches and pulp from our lumber harbor we shall make the finest white paper. If the Fox River Valley can import rags from Egypt, we can. If Holland can make the best paper importing **all** the raw material, we can go it one better.

95

Louisiana is the most important fur market of the United States; tannin and mangrove bark are brought in from Latin America. Should we not have the fur industry of America located here? Hides from Argentine, artificial leather from our celluloid, with raw hides imported, with a proper developed tanning industry here using imported tanning bark, should not the Industrial Canal be a center of shoe industry if our cotton fiber together with our oil gives us the basic coating for the best grade of patent leather. The same cotton fibre gives us pegamoid for bookbinding. Should we not have the manufactory of books here with our fine paper industry and the lithographic stone from nearby states?

Instances might be multiplied without end. It is obvious that manufacturers will not continue under disadvantages of transportation. Linoleum can nowhere in America be made cheaper than right on the banks of the Industrial Canal. Northern Africa can give us the cork, Argentine the linseed oil, the burlap from India. Can any other harbor of the United States assemble these raw materials cheaper than we? Can any other harbor offer an easier approach to as many markets as we, be they domestic or foreign?

New Orleans, with our water-borne Kentucky, Illinois and Alabama coal, should be a leading coal export harbor.

The Government's most important and safest navy yard should be located between the Government Army Supply Base and the lock, behind the lock and between the lock and the warehouse harbor.

The fisheries of the Gulf coast produced in 1918 marine products to a value of $6,500,000, of which shrimp and oysters, red snappers and other local fish made up $4,000,000. The warm water of the Gulf abounds in a much greater number of different species of food fish than are to be found in the colder currents of the North Atlantic. And although the canning shrimp and oyster industry has developed to the considerable proportions and with a little catering to would surely become of much greater importance, we lack here every vestige of accommodation to our fishing industry. Would not an efficient fish harbor draw all this industry to New Orleans with its magnificent railroad system to the rear? And shipping facilities to the other parts of the world?

These then are some of the industries which must find a location on the Industrial Canal to an advantage. But these are by no means all. With proper planning and developing the key industries will bring many other factories in their wake.

Seeking the very same advantages as the steel plants, attracted by cheap steel breaking ''Pittsburgh plus'', factories and plants, now shipping their products for exports made elsewhere through New Orleans, will come to the Industrial Canal locating around various centers which may be called commodity harbors.

The blast furnaces as key industry in the steel harbor must bring coke-by-product plant, foundries, cast iron pipe factories, stoves, radiators, stuctural steel plants, nuts and bolts, nails, wire cables, barbed wire, wrought iron pipe, pipe fittings, chains and railway track material now exported through New Orleans at the rate of 250,000 tons last year and a value of $25,000,000.

Further, the blast furnaces must force the creation of fabricating plants, agricultural implements, railroad equipment, elevators, conveyors, cranes, tanks and fans, machinery, pumps, compressors, contractors' materials, engines, excavating machinery, flour mills, laundry machinery, machine tools, mining, sugar, rice mill, textile, saw mill, woodworking, and refrigerating machinery, printing presses, windmills and sewing machines.

Together with the other material at hand we shall see here arise plants producing tin plate, enamel ware, galvanizing, screens, springs, hardware, iron hoops and barrels.

All of which must be followed by the location of shipyards for ocean and shallow draft vessels, barges, lighters, dredges, etc., and automobile bodies and parts.

Thought must be given while reading this, to the very important factor that for once in the world's history we have the unique opportunity to so locate each industry that it derives the maximum advantages from this location through the juxtaposition of allied industries from which it must draw its raw resources and to which it may sell its by-products or finished products, and this all at a minimum cost of transportation and handling. Invariably it should be possible to either receive or deliver its products out or into the Industrial Harbor or chiefly from or to Louisiana, or from or to other markets at the choice of water or rail service and much of that.

These factories should be bound up in six branches of the steel harbor, the pig iron, cast iron, fabricating, machinery, process and construction harbor.

97

This group of six harbors are bound to find quick occupants, predicated upon two conditions: first the Dock Board must not block such natural development in any manner; second, the steel harbor must materialize. Granting the first, the second will surely follow. No power can stop it.

An efficient and economical steel harbor may be built upon a strip of land 10,000 feet wide, 18,000 feet long, connected with the Industrial Canal by a lateral 500 feet wide which reaches clear to the rear boundary line. The pig iron harbor to be a double branch 500 feet wide commencing 1,000 feet back on the lateral figured from the front boundary line, making a 45 degrees angle with the lateral, leaning towards the rear. The steel harbor to run parallel to this, commencing 2,000 feet more to the rear. The same to be the case for the cast iron harbor, fabrication harbor and process harbor, while the construction harbor should be square upon the lateral 1,000 feet from the rear boundary lines. All the side laterals to stop 800 feet from the longitudinal boundary lines with the exception of the cast iron harbor which at one side reaches out directly to the deep sea channel in the lake and on the other side of the chemical harbor.

Between the steel harbor and the Industrial Canal the lumber harbor should be located.

Each of these groups is fully able and warranted through economy gained to pay $2,000,000 for a lateral and $6,000,000 for 600 acres at $10,000 per acre, and $1,000,000 for dredging and revetment, as each harbor group of industries needs only to give in total a saving of $800,000 a year to justify such expenditure.

Such steel harbor would cost $12,000,000 for laterals and covering 4,094 acres, $40,900,000 in Dock Board harbor fees outside of the cost of the real estate, dredging and revetment work. The dredging and revetment would figure at about $9,100,000, so that the entire harbor would cost $62,000,000 outside of the land value, or about $15,200 per acre, plus the real estate, road improvements, relaying of railroad tracks, etc., about $20,000 per acre in total, or $82,000,000, which means that when this harbor is fully developed and all the industries are located and developed the economy margin must be sufficient to permit such investment and still hold out sufficient inducement to bring the industries to locate in this harbor.

This entire harbor has 150,000 lineal feet of deep sea frontage, each lineal foot giving land in average 1,200 feet deep. A safe harbor open to all means of transportation most economically brought together, absolute freedom in development, no harbor dues or charge of whatsoever nature, easy access to raw material, markets, demand for work and by-products, all for $547 per lineal frontal foot (less per acre than the average real estate values of the warehouses of New Orleans,) land directly connected with allied industries, ocean, lake, river, canal, dray, rail, barge line, lighterage.

The payments for laterals should be used for funding to meet the maintenance of the harbors. The benefit of New Orleans will be to have all of these industries brought here, increasing assessed tax valuation, value of real estate and every kind of business, while as soon as the canal and river bonds are paid off the revenue of $10,000 an acre will bring substantial capital into the Dock Board treasury.

The total steel groups mentioned before exported out of the Gulf ports a total of 11,500,000 tons. In this harbor a saving of at least $3 per ton or $34,500,000 can be created—about 40% of the entire capital involved.

Of course, each commodity harbor can be started in a modest way. The real estate owners may form groups with Dock Board's approval, paying the Dock Board in a lump sum for the lateral right, or the Dock Board may charge each industry a specified ratio of the lateral charge fixing excessive tolls to such plants not meeting this charge. This general statement holds of course not only for the metal group but also for any of the succeeding groups.

It must be seen to that each lateral has a broad field behind and around it. This means that ample space is left between each lateral and each lateral should be planned to reach as far into the back country as possible.

A second commodity harbor should be the lumber harbor, to be located 800 feet from the canal between the canal and the steel harbor connected with both by the same lateral. A lumber harbor in which lumber may be received and stored floating or on shore, sawed, creosoted, timber and lumber from the west, tropics, east or environments. The following industries come under this group: import and export, sawmill, sash and doors, boxing, moulding,

99

veneering, handles, staves, ties, cooperage, cisterns, furniture, pulp, paper, beaver-board, shingles, matches, rosin, turpentine, tar and pitch.

A harbor as seen in fig.— would contain 350 acres of floating storage and 440 acres of land storage and 80 acres of factory sites, consisting of six triangular segments with deep water on each side.

Such harbor, 890 acres in all, including lateral right, acreage lien, real estate, dredging and revetment, would cost $15,200,000, or about $17,500 per acre, or $550 per lineal foot with an average acre consisting of half land. one quarter deep water, one quarter shallow pond space; making the cost of $1,400,000 for the factory sites and $13,800,000 for the twelve lumber sites or $1,150,000 for each lumber yard. Each such lumber site has 1,125 feet of deep sea harbor frontage, 14 acres of shallow storage pond and 36 acres of land storage, freedom henceforth of any harbor or dock charges, sufficient storage for 80 million feet of land storage and 7 million feet of water storage. Last year New Orleans imported and exported 200 million feet of lumber and $7,000,000 of wood products.

There are further in this harbor 180 acres of factory sites with a total of 7,500 lineal feet of deep sea frontage for $186 per lineal foot, each foot being 1,056 deep in average—17½ᶜ per square foot for factory site, ($7,778 per acre) forever free from any harbor charges, all and the best transportation facilities, certainly a great drawing card.

The factories could be grouped in six groups as follows:

I. Ties, staves, handles, and sash and doors.

II. Cooperage and cisterns

III. Veneering, moulding, matches, shingles, lath and boxes

IV. Pulp, beaver-board and paper

V. Furniture.

VI. Naval stores, rosin, tar, turpentine, pitch and creosoting.

In such manner it should not be difficult to secure such factories on these sites within thirty years, each free from harbor charges, ideal site and transportation with raw materials capable of being floated to them at cost, not much higher than loading or unloading them.

The above gives an idea of what can be done.

Other harbors are the oil harbor with the opportunity for fuel refineries, dye industries and wood preservers and roofing paper,

the chemical harbor which in addition to the industries already named should find room for plants producing toilet articles, washing powder, drugs, chewing gum, paints, inks, etc.; the coal harbor with her coke ovens and solvay plant, the leather harbor with furs, hides, belting, shoes, saddles, as center; the clothing harbor housing the factories for overalls, gloves, hats, textiles, collars and ivory buttons; the rubber harbor with tires, shoes and rain coats as products; the cordage harbor, with provisions for fiber, oakum, burlap, tents, awnings, sails, etc.; the stockyard harbor; the canning harbor for corn products, canned goods; molasses, etc.; the fish harbor with canning for oysters, shrimp, and crushed shells; the food harbor for breadstuffs and other grain products, candy, chocolates, spaghetti, macaroni, biscuits, margarine, cocoa, animal oils, vegetable oils, soft drinks, etc., etc.; the fruit harbor, power harbor and others.

The oil harbor should be located east of the steel harbor and not connected with same, having entrance from the lake, connected across the river with pipe line.

The coal harbor should be located between the steel and oil harbor, connected with the steel harbor.

The central power plant should be located between Bayou Bienvenue and the L. & N. R. R. as near to the canal as possible, with a 50% supporting station on the west side of the canal. These power plants should be built of the universal type so that increasing the capacity becomes a simple matter.

We have seen now what opportunities we can offer the industrial world in locating in this Industrial Canal zone, which industries can avail themselves of these opportunities, how a price for real estate favorably comparing with other factory sites may secure these advantages and opportunities for these industries. The question of how many of these industries and in what period will avail themselves of this opportunity remains now to be answered.

The capital invested in manufacturing enterprise in the United States increased from $8,975,256,496 in 1899, and $22,790,979,937 in 1914. This is an average increase of 10% each year or 150% every ten.

Since the new waterway of Rotterdam was opened in 1873, its commerce more than doubled every ten years, so that in 1913 it was eighteen times the amount of 1873.

Our Latin American trade grew from 75 million dollars in 1895 to 1,500 million dollars in 1920, twenty-folded itself in twenty-five years.

Our domestic trade increased from nine billion dollars in 1895 to 93 billions in 1920, ten-folded itself in twenty-five years.

Is it not a justifiable hope to expect that, where we offer a truly unparalleled opportunity, advantages that must weigh heavier than any other consideration, a very large share of all new industries created in the United States in the next twenty years will come to the Industrial Canal?

No doubt can be entertained that granting a good practical plan, well conceived, ably executed, with efficient selling organization, armed with facts, knowledge, maps, statistics, models, reports, and other data, such organization should dispose of at least 300 acres in average for the next twenty years (3 extra years to pay for the cost of selling) growing in impetus as the plans are executed until by 1940 the land will go under demand growing under its own momentum.

London did not hesitate to build and finish this year the Royal Albert Dock in the city itself only 6½ miles away from the Bank of England, costing $22,000,000 giving only 64 acres and 10 000 lineal feet of wharves giving space for about fourteen steamers. The dock is equipped with twenty-four three-ton cranes. The lock has only one gate and is 45 feet deep, 100 feet wide and 800 feet clear length, with a possible extension in length by caisson of 100 feet.

Rotterdam spent 34 million dollars for an artificial channel better than the Rhine could give.

38 million dollars were spent to give Amsterdam, a harbor smaller than New Orleans, a good channel to the sea.

Manchester spent 80 million dollars for a sea connection. Brugge, Ghent and many other ports can give proof that $25,000,-000 for our industrial Canal must be a paying enterprise.

But if ever any enterprise needed a plan, surely this Industrial Canal for which we have no standards to go by but for the future of which we must depend very largely upon what plan we adopt and how we execute it, needs one.

The plan must be made by competent men, provide for a long period and be of sufficient flexibility to meet changing conditions in commerce, engineering and science, yet be rigid enough to enforce its dictums.

The plan must be made by competent men. Who are they? Selected business men called into consultation, are able enough to advise if they will agree to devote their entire time to the problem and after they have given years of study to the problem, New Orleans could safely rely upon the plan adopted by them. But as a by-play, devoting their spare time in developing such plan, even in advisory capacity, their suggestion cannot carry much weight.

The port and terminal problem is one for both engineers and economists.

I believe that the plan should be made in such a manner that the greatest amount of engineering talent, scientists, harbor experts, economists, statisticians, terminal and railroad men, and transportation and shipping men aid in developing the plan.

This can be done by inviting the national engineering societies, civil, electrical, mechanical, mining, metallurgical, marine naval architects. etc., etc.; the terminal and port associations, etc., etc.; the shipping and forwarding and industrial organizations etc., etc.; to make a diligent research into the matter, hold lectures, hearings, debates and researchings until they are ready to advise what from their point of view should be done and is considered essential, to take the fullest advantage of this virgin opportunity offered. The dock board can offer each society a substantial premium, say of 15 or 20 thousand dollars in prizes to be awarded by the society itself for the best paper or papers, and $5,000 for research work and putting the combined and adopted recommendations in concise form before the clearing house committee. This committee to be made up of a member of the Dock Board, the General Manager, and the man or men who will be charged with carrying out the plan. This committee must have ample time, funds and talent at their disposal to consolidate the recommendations made and finally lay before the Dock Board a finished plan. Such report should be published and sent broadcast with the request for written criticism. Then upon that data and information the Dock Board can safely adopt a fixed plan and policy for the use of the Industrial Canal.

The formation of such plan should be given all the time required. The formation of a plan should have started with the digging of the canal.

I believe that the letters to the various societies, associations and organizaiions should be accompanied by a very clear expose of the problem at hand.

The Dock Board should lay down some general rules and instructions to govern those that are active in developing a plan, some of which are:

I. It should fix the period in which it must be relied upon that all expenses are repaid by the canal beneficiaries.

II. The six principles named on page 6 must be followed.

III. A fund should be created and perpetuated to maintain the industrial zone.

IV. Provision should be made for the use of the surplus funds, one of which may be an agreement to repay the Government out of the surplus fund for the new lake channel.

V. Care should be exercised that the economic margin is not destroyed through too heavy burdens.

This economic margin should be large enough to pay its fair proportion of the Industrial Canal and maintenance funds, to pay for the harbor work, to pay for the land with substantial profit to the owner and leave ample margin of economy to bring the industries to the industrial zone.

VI. It should provide for such machinery that at any time for good cause shown corrections or alterations can be made without destroying the usefulness of the plan.

VII. It should take care that the owners of surrounding real estate do not solely reap the benefit of the Industrial Canal work but share the advantages as per V.

VIII. It should be made impossible for any one to reap the advantages of the Canal without due contribution to its funds; for instance by extending the Dock Board limits further in the Parish of St. Bernard and by forbidding the creation of harbor sites without the Dock Board's approval.

IX. The plan should purport to see at least three or more centuries into the future as for instance, the city of Washington, so that we do not need to follow Paris' example, which had to spend $200,000,000 in correcting her street plan because some one a few centuries ago had no vision and optimism enough to adopt and lay out a city plan going far enough into the future.

X. The plan must give ways and means to force the execution of it and see that no land owners in any way move away or deviate from this plan.

XI. Care should be taken that each industry is so located as to give the maximum of support to others and derive the maximum of support from them.

XII. All plans should be solely based upon private development.

XIII. The report should clearly show which are the key industries and why, so that they may be secured first and bring their by-product factories in their wake. Some of these key industries are: pig iron, lumber import and export, dye industries, etc.

These should be some of the guiding thoughts for those that occupy themselves with formulating a plan. The plan itself may carry out many varying principles. However, to attempt to make the canal itself pay must be forborne.

The canal is five and one-third miles long, but could give only 46,000 feet avaible frontage on account of the location of the lock, of which 46,000 feet already 7,100 feet, or 15½ % are squandered, increasing the necessary charges over the remaining 38,900 feet over 17%.

If thirty years would be required to bring the use of the canal up to its capacity and the necessary provision is made for the river bonds, the total sum the canal must bring is $96,000,000, or about $2,500 per lineal foot, or figuring on the usable available depth of the land behind, would mean $178,000 per acre.

To charge per ton must be forthwith dismissed. The canal must be free from tolls; otherwise the Government will make one, or the Lake Borgne Canal will become one. Besides the tonnage charges not permitting a funding payment as in the case of a fixed levee on the land cannot prevent a large deficit in operation in the first years, the very time large payments should be secured to avoid that the accumulated interest destroys the economic advantage of the canal. It seems sure to me that tolls higher than 20^c per ton cannot be enforced and the canal cost with accumulated interest would double itself in the first eleven years as the tolls during that period would hardly have paid for the operating cost. Besides, it would permit the real estate owners materially to delay the development through excessive demands for the land. Canal rental and tolls combined won't work because some industries would require much land for very little tonnage; others, very little land for very much tonnage, so that this would be discrim-

105

nation since one would pay more than the other for the use of the canal, keeping some away and we need and want every industry we can get.

There are about 100,000 acres north of Bayou Bienvenue, east of the canal, west of the Rigolets, virgin swamp land that can be turned into harbor land. Each acre paying $10,000 would give a total of $1,000,000,000. The answer to the question, "Can it pay?" is easy.

The value of land depends upon the income it will yield in connection with the application of capital and labor.

The plan should answer such questions as the following:

Is it wise to have one site only for one industry? Even if one firm takes it entirely? Is it correct to provide in the general rules, regulations of sales methods, such as forbidding the sale of steel manufactured on the canal on the basis of "Pittsburg plus?"

What general rules and regulations regarding the operation of the canal, such as those relating to speed of navigation, what craft or freight should be prohibited from entering lock or canal, etc., should be adopted?

What laws are needed, if any?

A law should be passed now designating, following the plan, what land should be harbor land and permit the fixing of its value, and the planned industry for a certain land to expropriate at the fixed price plus accrued and accumulated interest less annual revenue. The owner to establish before the canal management yearly what this interest less revenue amounts to.

The adopted plan should receive the necessary legal status approved by test suits in the highest court.

For the sake of New Orleans taxpayers who paid for the Canal, the Parish limits should be extended to include all potential harbor land so that the increase in tax valuation comes to the relief of New Orleans. Until this is done, the Dock Board should not permit the digging of laterals leading into St. Bernard Parish unless the Parish will in some manner compensate the parish of Orleans.

Some other legal corrections are needed, such as the tax levies. One great hardship on industries located in Louisiana are the State taxes, which are typical taxes of an agricultural State and not an industrial state. A tax on raw materials does not kill the goose that lays the golden eggs, but kills its mother before the

brood's birth. With this tax removed it is safe to predict that many fold more tax moneys can be collected than this vandal's tax on raw materials and supplies now yields.

Tax exemption means nothing. No industry that cannot or will not pay its fair share of the public burden should be wanted, but annihilating taxes should not be raised.

In addition to this purchase price the industry should pay the real estate owner either a lump sum per acre fixed by law, for unearned increment or the land owner to have always first right in creating the designated industry on his land himself, making the required payment to the Dock Board, commencing work within a fixed period.

Another question that must be investigated and answered is: Should there be any variation in contribution per acre varying with the location? I believe the answer may be "yes," charging a little more for land near lakes and bayous and less for strictly interior land, such variation to compensate for the dredging of a channel to place the land on parity. Again others may hold to the contrary, contending that the natural value that is the basic value of the land will take care of this.

It may prove to be a wise policy to hold out special inducement to early comers, say in selection and in price as the more land sold the first year, the easier the financial burden of the canal.

If the legal obstructions that make it impossible for the Dock Board to sell again land bought for selling purposes cannot be removed, a private company may be formed with the Dock Board's backing and under its control. This company may buy the land to hold it for the plan's purpose.

Finally, it is entirely possible to form a private company that will carry out one of such plans with the Dock Board's approval, cooperation and supervision. Should the Board seek this, the private company should repay all canal investments, interest and share with the Dock Board part of its profits. Again, such company could be formed as agent for the Dock Board very much along the lines of the Shipping Board and the United States. Such company may own its lighters, maintain a joint traffic organization, operate the canal, carry on a selling and advertising campaign and even operate exhibition ships.

107

The Dock Board has full authority to deny harbor facilities or location to any land not approved by it, so that no one may reap undue benefits from the canal without meeting under some provision a part of the Canal's expense.

All railroad service must be rendered solely by the Public Belt, and all private railroads should stop short of the land under Dock Board's authority. Old tracks to be removed and new laid following the recommendations of the adop'ed plan.

This Industrial Canal will see development of a proper lighterage system, wharfingers, floating grain elevators, fuel colliers and floating cranes.

The residential part of the town is to remain to the west of the canal, the workmen's dwelling artistically planned behind and around each industry.

When the canal is brought to proper development, New Orleans is going to be the port of the greatest dispatch, the cheapest fueling port, the port with the largest hinterland, with the largest markets, and deposits, the largest industrial port, the port with the largest, longest and the widest system of used waterways and be, in fact, the largest port of the world.

When that day has arrived, and the Industrial Canal has done its full duty we shall have on the river front a public controlled harbor with free wharfage except for labor charges the only charges made.

The city itself through large influx of taxes will have municipally owned, cheaply sold, or freely given, light, power, telephone, trolley cars, markets, sewer and water service, paid for out of $20,000,000 raised out of the $2,000,000,000 assessed valuation of the plants on the Industrial Canal.

Let us all through community of interest, promise to help to realize that destiny with unity of purpose and cooperation in action. Go where you will, east, north, west or south, you will hear the same refrain: "Of all the cities in the world, New Orleans has the greatest prospects for future growth and development."

This then is New Orleans opportunity as transcribed in the proper use of the Industrial Canal and Inner Harbor.

COMPOSITION and Presswork by
first year students of the Printing
Dept., Isaac Delgado Central Trades
School, New Orleans.

CPSIA information can be obtained
at www.ICGtesting.com
Printed in the USA
LVHW061628230323
742417LV00002B/24